EMBROIDERY COMPANION

EMBROIDERY COMPANION

CLASSIC DESIGNS FOR MODERN LIVING

*30 Projects in Decorative Embroidery,
Counted Cross Stitch, and Crewelwork*

alicia paulson

Creator of Posie Gets Cozy and Author of *Stitched in Time*

POTTER
CRAFT

NEW YORK

Published in the United States by Potter Craft,
an imprint of the Crown Publishing Group,
a division of Random House, Inc., New York.
www.crownpublishing.com
wwww.pottercraft.com

POTTER CRAFT and colophon is a registered
trademark of Random House, Inc.

Library of Congress Cataloging-in-Publication Data
Paulson, Alicia.
 Embroidery companion : classic designs for modern
living : 30 projects in decorative embroidery, cross stitch,
and crewelwork / by Alicia Paulson.
    p. cm.
 Includes index.
 ISBN 978-0-307-46235-0
 1. Embroidery--Patterns. I. Title.
 TT771.P367 2009
 746.44'041--dc22

                    2010003102

Printed in China
10 9 8 7 6 5 4 3 2 1
First Edition

Photography & Illustrations
by Alicia Paulson

Technical Editing
by Karyn Gerhard

Styling by Alicia Paulson
& Andrea Corrona Jenkins

Book Design by Chalkley Calderwood

For Andy

WHO HEALS HEARTS,
WHO HEALED MINE.

Contents

Preface

I don't remember actually learning to embroider, but when I unravel the skein of my childhood memories there is a tiny brown horse standing in a green field against the blue sky of a July afternoon. I spent a hundred hours with him, I'm sure—moving from quiet room to quiet room in my grandparents' air-conditioned '50s ranch-style home: Sneaking into my grandpa's screened porch when he wasn't there watching wrestling on his little black-and-white TV; settling myself under the tree at the far end of the backyard near the railroad trestle and ragweed-covered embankment that bordered the property—everywhere I went, I took my little bay horse. He was painted on a square of needlepoint canvas, and very portable.

His scene was the one I imagined myself into a thousand times; with each completed stitch, he and his pastoral world grew, dense and colorful. If I closed my eyes, I could feel his velvet nostrils, soft and whiskery as wool.

That summer I was nine, and our mother had gone back to work, so our dad's parents watched my sisters and me during the day. The canvas was part of a needlepoint kit I'd gotten at Weiboldt's department store, back when they carried fabric and sewing supplies (back when they still existed at all). It was purchased for me by my mom as my summer project, a way to assuage the boredom of long, quiet suburban days spent at our grandparents' place, away from our school and neighborhood friends. I picked the project more for the horse than for the needlepoint: Almost every object I owned was decorated with a horse, a horse head, or a horseshoe. Needlework couldn't have had a better ambassador than that canvas Thoroughbred.

⋄ ⋄ ⋄

Twenty years later, embroidery re-entered my life during another summer filled with long, quiet (too long, too quiet) afternoons. The previous spring, I had been the pedestrian in a serious pedestrian-truck accident. Over several brutal months, many medical professionals worked to stitch back together my destroyed foot, now a Frankensteinian patchwork of muscle, blood vessel, and nerve. I spent my twenty-ninth summer in bed, recovering from the many surgeries I'd needed and willing myself to wander in imaginary locations: on television, where I watched the Travel Channel for half-hour upon exotic half-hour; in books, where my preoccupied mind couldn't keep the characters or settings straight; and in embroidery, where I stitched flower beds of floss blossoms across the hems of too many sheets and pillowcases to remember. In far away places, I escaped the reality of my own uncertain and unhappy days.

But embroidery was my best travel agent—and doctor. Through almost every moment of almost every day of my recovery, I stitched a wonderland of hearts and flowers. Each morning I set about creating the world I wanted, so different from the real one I was in. Each night I fell asleep with a tiny garden in my hand. As soon as I finished one thing, I started another. The minute I started another, I began dreaming of the next. Tick. Tock. Tick. Tock. Stitch. Stitch. Stitch. The sun came up. The sun went down. Stitch, stitch, stitch. Days and weeks and months went by. Outside my window, there was evidence that the season was changing: Real blossoms budded, bloomed, and left. But for me, with the end of my leg caged by bandage and the framework of a metal fixator holding bones in place, every day felt endless, and the same. It seemed

new leaf, I grew. Within the year, I was back on my fragile, uncertain feet.

Today, ten years later, I walk. Embroidery—though done with less desperation (most days!)—is still a central part of my busy life. Most days are filled with the business of sewing, and most evenings begin on the sofa with a needle and some kind of thread in hand. There is never a time when I don't have a project in the hoop. Though crafting is now my work, embroidery is still my first love.

❖ ❖ ❖

that time would never start. There was only me, and the hoop, and the fabric. I would never run out of thread.

But something was happening: As I stitched, bones knit. Transplanted muscle grabbed on. New skin scabbed over and sprouted. Blood vessels bred more vessels, and at the end of my leg, a sort-of foot appeared. Though on a steady drip of painkillers, cable TV, and solicited encouragement from anyone who happened to be within range, only embroidery seemed able to tap me into that special state of consciousness where I was soothed and in control; where I felt, and eventually truly believed, that everything would be all right. It was not a metaphor, back then; with every

Special moments happen when you use special items. Imagining special moments is all it takes to begin the process of creating more of them—think of the candlelit desserts with friends who will rumple your embroidered napkins, the chubby baby who might dribble peaches on her cross-stitched strawberry bib, the cold (now warm) nights you'll spend snuggling under your personalized blanket. I've planned dinner parties just because I was excited about using a newly embroidered tablecloth, I have to admit. I think there was food there (surely I must have fed people *something*); the company—and the table—were *wonderful*. There is such enormous satisfaction in using things you've created yourself, especially now that we are all, collectively, striving to become more conscious of the provenance—and the potential future—of the products we use and consume. You'll be much more likely to keep, treasure, and pass on things that have been made with fine materials and created with care.

But what I love most about embroidering is the physical effect that doing it has on my body: blood pressure goes down, worries fade, breathing evens, mind stops racing with thoughts of all that needs doing. Practicing embroidery gives your body and your brain a chance to slow down and stitch itself back together after a long day, or a long year. This, I believe, is its true appeal. In the years since my accident, I can't even count how many people have told me that doing handwork has saved them; I know it saved me.

Embroidery is just good medicine for so much of what ails us in the modern world. Think of this book as inspiration for creating a slower, prettier, less hectic, more special version of your very own little corner of the world—and maybe even (who knows?) your life.

Introduction

Embroidery, in its most technical sense, is "the embellishment of cloth with stitching." It's a simple and (ironically) unromantic definition for what can be such an exquisitely sophisticated medium. When needle and thread are used to decorate even the most humble of fabrics, something magical happens, and has been happening for thousands of years. Embroidery exists in every culture where people sew, and evidence of our apparent human need to create stitched ornamentation—from the simplest cross-stitched folk motif to the most intricate satin-stitched monogram—reaches through centuries and across borders. Tell someone you embroider—even someone who has never picked up a needle—and they can invariably tell *you* something about the silk-stitched tapestry they picked up while traveling in China, the chicken scratch tablecloth handed down from their grandma in Iowa, or the lovingly smocked bodice of a baby dress, kept pristine all these years.

That's because there is just something special about embroidery done by hand, and anyone can recognize the imprint of a person—not a machine—in it. Charming or whimsical or regal or colorful, it is also a record of things. In the design the stitcher chose, in the colors she (or he) used, in the stitches she worked, and in the fibers she handled, there exists a portrait of a time and place, a personality, and the thoughts of many quiet hours. Rarely is hand embroidery done simply for the finished piece itself. Its pleasures are in its choices and rhythms, mistakes and discoveries. Look at it closely—in all its perfection and its mistakes—and you will see someone in it, and see what they loved.

Embroidery Companion showcases thirty of my domestically inclined dream projects. It is a collection of designs influenced and inspired by so many of my favorite things: the bright garlands of Hungarian peasant dresses, the folksy charm of Ukrainian cross-stitch borders, the earnest beauty of natural wildflowers and woodland flora, the sophistication of vintage French monograms, the sweet simplicity of early American motifs, the spare modernism of Scandinavian design, even the old-fashioned whimsy of my own modern housewares. This is just all the stuff *I* truly love, expressed in needle and thread.

Organized into three sections—decorative embroidery, counted cross-stitch, and crewelwork—the projects are accompanied by photos of finished items, stitch charts and colorways, templates and stitch symbols, and instructions for finishing. At the beginning of each section, I'll explain the basics, and suggest types of fabrics, kinds of floss, and sizes of needles to use.

Within each section, the projects vary in skill level, though the Easy, Medium, and Difficult indications I've included for both the embroidery and the finishing are only suggestions. As far as embroidery goes:

- ❖ "EASY" projects are appropriate for beginners and feature simple design templates or basic, uncomplicated motifs.
- ❖ "MEDIUM" projects are best for stitchers who are familiar with the basics, but are ready for a longer-term commitment and a bigger project, with more involved templates and larger, more intricate charts.

- ❖ "DIFFICULT" projects are physically larger and require an ease with all transfer methods, chart reading, and stitches.

To finish the projects, I've presumed a basic familiarity with general sewing techniques, including basic machine-stitching, pressing, hemming, gathering, and hand-stitching.

- ❖ "EASY" projects require little to no finishing besides cleaning, pressing, and framing.
- ❖ "MEDIUM" projects will have you doing a bit of measuring, hemming, basting, and gathering.
- ❖ "DIFFICULT" projects require experience with more complicated techniques involved in apparel sewing or quilting.

If finishing things feels daunting to you, contact your local fabric store for referrals to local seamstresses who can assist you with sewing your projects into finished pieces. Some embroiderers don't do any of their own finishing, and there's something to be said for giving yourself permission to focus most of your effort only on those parts of making things that you really enjoy.

Embroidery takes more patience than skill; if you're just starting, my advice is, as always, to fall in love first. Pick the project you love, not the one that looks easiest or the one that seems like it'll go fast, and start small. Maybe instead of five large motifs along the hem of the Harvest Apron (page 72), you do just one; or perhaps outline the large, looping monogram of the Petal Pillowcases (page 58) in backstitch, saving satin-stitch practice just for the blossoms and not the entire initial. As your confidence improves, you'll see that practice truly does make more-perfect when it comes to embroidery. (I never say "perfect," because I don't believe in it, and anyway, enjoyment, not perfection, is my goal.) Enjoy the ambling pace and the process of learning-by-doing—there is no prize for speed-stitching, nor any substitute for the experience of simply pulling needle through thread, over and over, as you get it right. Just start, and have fun. Your pleasure will organically lead to an ever-increasing set of skills and abilities, all without your even realizing.

Basic Tools and Techniques

In this section you will find information about how to transfer template designs, what tools to have in your sewing box, and which general embroidery techniques you'll need to get stitching. At the back of the book you'll find an illustrated stitch glossary that includes all of the stitches used in the projects, a section on general sewing techniques, information about finishing and framing, and a list of inspiring sources to help you find everything you need to make what I've designed. Embroidery is a traditional but also ever-changing art form; just as old designs can be given new life with fresh treatments, new tools, fabrics, threads, and transfer techniques are constantly evolving. And though each stitcher also develops her own preferences and methods, these are some of my preferred tools and techniques to get you going in the right direction.

Templates

For the decorative embroidery and crewelwork projects in this book, you will find a corresponding line-art template (or set of templates) for each. Some templates may need to be enlarged on a copy machine to the percentage specified before transferring *only* the black outlines (and not the stitch symbols) to your fabric. To read these templates while stitching, just carefully follow the arrows pointing to outlines or filled spaces. Call-outs indicate the particular color number of thread to use, and an abbreviation of stitch type follows; stitch symbols are also indicated within fill areas, and their direction can help guide you to orient your stitches properly. And don't forget that when your muse directs you to change any of it, follow her call. Adding your own touches makes a piece truly yours.

Abbreviations found in the templates refer to the following types of stitches I've used. Please refer to the Illustrated Stitch Guide (page 148) for directions on how to execute stitches.

Abbreviations

RS = Running stitch

BS = Back stitch

TS = Stem stitch

SS = Satin stitch

PSS = Padded satin stitch

LSS = Long and short stitch

FS = Fly Stitch

CS = Chain stitch

LD = Lazy daisy stitch

FK = French knot

LS = Blanket stitch

CT = Couched trellis

XS = Cross-stitch

DXS = Double cross-stitch

WCS = Woven circle stitch

Appleton Crewel Wool

Six-Strand Floss

Perle Cotton #3

3609

.601

732
(731)

597

321

Perle Cotton #5

Transferring Designs

Transferring the design is my least-favorite part of any embroidery project, since it often requires you to trace, measure, or otherwise generally fuss in an you've-only-got-this-one-chance-to-get-it-right sort of way (the pressure!). But over the years I've learned that this important step can be made much easier if you become comfortable with the various methods of transferring templates to fabric, choose your tools carefully, and then just take a deep breath—rushing here is not advised, since taking your time to get this step right will have far-reaching effects on your happiness with both the process of stitching and the final product.

And before you do anything, don't forget to determine whether your finished item is going to ultimately be washed and dried regularly or not. If it will be, you should wash and dry the fabric before doing any design transferring or stitching. Use the temperatures and the (mild) detergent you will be using once the item is being used, and wash and dry according to fabric manufacturer's recommendations. When pressing, test the temperature of your iron on a scrap of fabric first; you want it hot enough to get out any wrinkles, but not so hot that you damage the fibers, so be careful and take your time when pressing fabrics you aren't familiar with.

When transferring designs, let your fabric dictate the method of transfer. For projects done on light-colored cotton or linen, my preferred method of transferring templates is to use a light source and a fine-tipped Micron marker—a permanent pen whose fine but dark line won't ever wash out—and just trace the design directly onto the fabric. I use a Sakura Pigma Micron marker with a 0.30mm or 0.45mm tip for everything I trace.

Tracing

In order to transfer a template by tracing, tape the template, right side up, to a bright window or a light box (more about these later), making sure it is level. Then simply place your fabric smoothly on top of the design, centering where necessary (a ruler can help here), and tape it in place, as well. Using the Micron marker, carefully trace the outline of the design you see through the fabric—just do the outline, and not the stitch symbols.

Let's go back to that word "permanent" in permanent pen, because I know you twitched a little bit when you read it. But let me explain. When transferring, I never use pencil (which smudges and looks dirty) or fabric markers that automatically fade or rinse out with a bit of water. Although you're safe being a little sloppy with them, it makes me crazy to have to race against time to complete the design before the lines disappear forever—and in my experience, even the markers that claim they need to be washed out often start fading on their own without the help of water. They're also hard to see on certain fabrics, and there's nothing I like less than struggling to figure out just *where* I'm supposed to put my stitches. Even one strand of floss can completely cover the thin line that a 0.30mm Micron marker makes, so there's really no danger that you will see ink on fabric in your final piece; just be sure to place your stitches on the outside of the line, so that you're covering it completely.

The only situations where this method doesn't work is when you are using a fabric that is either too heavy to see through, even with a light source behind it, or too dark colored to make tracing a black line easy.

Iron-on Transfer Pencil

If the fabric is too heavy to trace on, I'll try using an iron-on transfer pencil first. (Test out a small design on a scrap of the same fabric to make sure it will work well before embarking on the whole design.) This special pencil can be purchased in the notions department of any fabric store, and contains a special "lead" that melts when it is heated. To use it, you must trace your design in reverse, since you will be placing it face down on your fabric to when ironing. Simply make a copy of the template onto regular copy paper at the size required and then place it, face down, on a light source. With firm pressure, trace the design with the iron-on transfer pencil onto the wrong side of the paper, creating a smooth, dark line. Cut the design from the paper, leaving a ¼" (6mm) margin, place it face down on the fabric, and press according to the manufacturer's directions for your particular pencil.

Dressmaker's Carbon Paper

A third method, which works on almost any fabric, is to use dressmaker's carbon paper. This special paper comes in various colors; choose a color that contrasts well with your fabric, and try to find paper that is chalk-based rather than wax-based—though the chalk paper is a bit messier, I have more success using it on most fabrics. To use it, place your fabric, right side up, on a hard surface. Lay the carbon paper, colored side down, on top of the fabric. Place the design (right side up) on top of the carbon paper, and trace, pressing hard, using a ballpoint pen. Be careful not to press the carbon paper anywhere other than on the design line, or the chalky surface with smudge onto your fabric. If that happens, just wash out any chalk with a bit of soap and water.

When transferring a simple design to a piece of thick, fuzzy wool, as with the hot water bottle covers on page 124, I think it's easiest to cut the simple motifs out of paper, then trace around them directly with a dressmaker's chalk pencil in a contrasting color.

❖ ❖ ❖

No matter which transfer method you choose, it's important to transfer the entire design at one time, as it is very difficult to realign features once the process has been interrupted. Trace it all at once, and be done.

If you find that you really enjoy embroidering, I urge you to consider investing in a light box and a small printer/scanner/photocopier the next time your computer's ink-jet printer is ready to be replaced. A light box is a box that contains an electric light source and has a frosted plastic surface; it transmits light through an image, making it easier to see. It is portable—pull it out and put it on your kitchen table when you need to use it. Though well-lit windows are available, light boxes make tracing large designs easier, since you won't have to be drawing on a vertical surface.

Ink-jet printers that double as scanners and photocopiers allow you to enlarge or reduce designs to your heart's content, right in the comfort of your own home. The convenience they offer is well worth the cost—and they're really quite affordable to begin with. It's such a luxury to be able to make color copies at home, too. When you start creating your own designs (and of course you will!), you'll be so happy to have this technology at your fingertips.

Tools to Have in Your Sewing Box

Hoops

Though several types of frames exist—from tabletop models to stationary stands—I've been embroidering quite happily for many years with nothing more complicated than a simple, inexpensive hoop. Consisting of two rings—an inner ring over which the fabric is stretched, then held taught by an outer ring tightened over it by a hefty screw—embroidery hoops are most often made of wood or plastic, and come in various sizes. If my design is small enough to fit entirely into a 5" (12.5cm) or 6" (15cm) hoop, I'll use it; otherwise I prefer to use a 4" (10cm) hoop because it fits most comfortably in my hand; if my piece is bigger than 4 inches (10 centimeters), I just move the hoop around the design, being careful not to crush the stitches I've already worked. To protect your fabric and allow it to be stretched more tightly without over-tightening the screw (and marring your stitches or warping the fabric irrevocably), wrap strips of lightweight cotton around the inner ring, and secure the ends with a few stitches.

Scissors

Without a doubt, you'll need a small, sharp pair of scissors made especially for embroidery. These make it easy to cut threads close to the back of your work, and, though it won't happen often, are invaluable when you need to take incorrectly worked stitches out. To finish many of the projects, you'll also need a pair of dressmaker's shears (and frequently, a rotary cutter, plastic ruler, and self-healing cutting mat).

Lighting

It's always best to embroider in good lighting. Real daylight is preferred, but a full-spectrum light source, which simulates daylight, can be used at night. If you're going to go off-trail and change colors from those listed for any project, or even try designing your own, it's imperative that you choose floss colors in real daylight, and not rely on any artificial—even full-spectrum—light source. Be aware, too, that when you're purchasing floss off the rack, the colors can look *vastly* different once you get them out from under the (usually) fluorescent bulbs at your local fabric store (spoken as one who has purchased green when trying to buy gray).

General Embroidery Techniques

Threading Needles

To thread my needle with either embroidery floss or crewel yarn, I moisten the end of the cut length of thread, then snip it at a 45-degree angle with sharp embroidery scissors. Then I hold the needle with the eye facing me, and feed the thread through it. Poor eyesight makes this process difficult for some; a needle threader, which can be purchased at any fabric store, will make threading easy.

Starting and Finishing Work

Knots are to be avoided in embroidery. To start your first stitches, take the needle from front to back, leaving a tail of thread a few inches long hanging toward the front of your piece. Work several small stitches over this tail, securing the thread and covering it completely with stitches for about ½" (13mm); clip off the long end, close to the work. If it's not possible to cover the tail with the starting stitches, leave a tail a few inches long hanging from the back, and run it under finished stitches on the back when possible; clip off the long end, close to the work. Try to run threads under stitches of the same color, and avoid running dark colors under light, lest they show through.

To finish off your thread, just run it under several stitches on the back, and snip the tail off close to the work.

Back of Work

Beginning embroiderers often fret about what the reverse side of their work looks like. The goal is, of course, to have the back of your work as neat and tidy as the front, but in my experience this is something that comes with time. If you're just starting out, don't worry too much about the back—just keep stitching. As your skills improve, you will begin to be able to "feel" whether something's going wrong on the back without even turning your work over. Knots and tangles are something you should always work to avoid, but if they happen, don't let it slow you down; if something's easy to fix, then practice fixing it, but if not, just let it go and keep stitching. It's more important that the front look good!

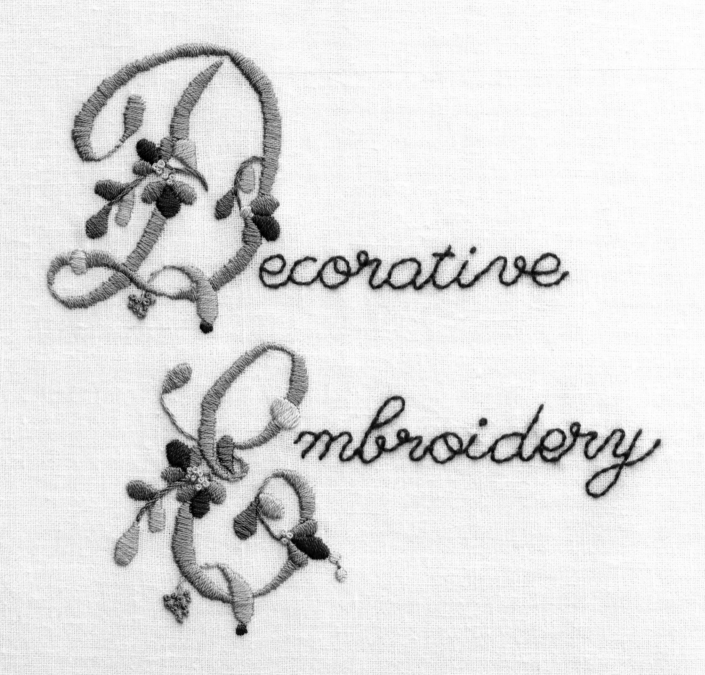

Decorative Embroidery

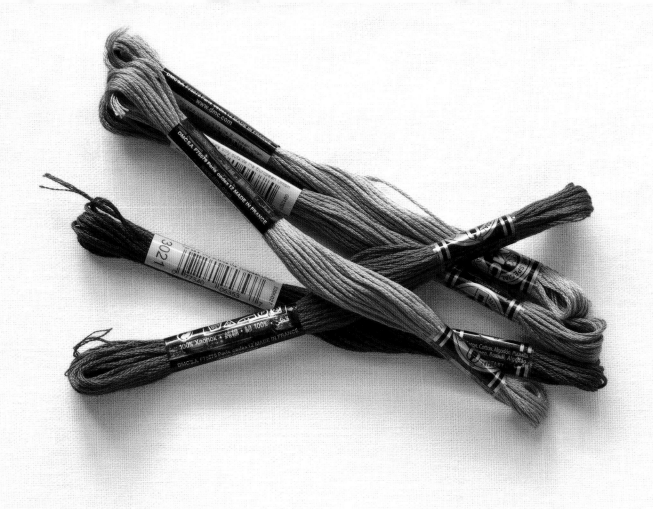

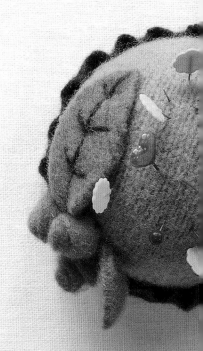

$\mathcal{W}$hat I call "decorative" embroidery requires transferring a line-art template to the fabric, then stitching either on or within the lines to create a design. Broadly speaking, it includes stitches and techniques from a plethora of traditions, and can range from simple backstitched outlines to realistic pictorials. Although there are myriad embroidery stitches you can learn, I've limited the ones I've used for the projects in this book to just over a dozen of the easiest and most widely used, showing that you can create wonderfully beautiful designs with just a few simple techniques.

Fabrics

Although virtually any type of fabric can be embroidered on, the choice of material used for decorative embroidery depends on the intended use of the finished piece. Detailed, delicate designs will show best on high-thread-count, finely woven fabrics; more loosely woven cloths work best with simple, rustic designs. In general, I like to embroider on smooth, high-thread-count cottons, linens, bamboos, and wool-blend felts. Almost all of the projects in this book are made of these beautiful, hard-wearing, natural fibers. If the piece is functional (like a pillowcase, dishtowel, or tablecloth) and going to be washed with use, it's *very* important to pre-wash and dry the fabric before you embroider it. Just use the soap, temperature, and wash-and-dry cycle settings you will be using on a regular laundry day, and follow any care instructions given by the manufacturer.

Threads

While almost any thread can be used for decorative embroidery, most of the decorative embroidery projects in this book use six-strand cotton floss, often just called "embroidery floss." Widely available in hundreds of beautiful, colorfast shades, embroidery floss is inexpensive and delivers a beautiful, glossy sheen. To use it, just tug on the end that gives a bit when pulled, and keep the paper bands intact; alternately, you can wind all of your skeins on plastic bobbins, then store them in boxes specifically designed to hold them (available at any craft store). Cut lengths of about 18" (45.5cm) to 24" (61cm)—any longer and you'll risk more tangling than stitching. To separate the six-strand length into plies, work strands away from each other at the center point of the length, and spread them apart toward either end of the strand. If you're using two or three strands for stitching, you can also separate individual strands before threading the needle (with all of them, again), as this separating and re-forming helps to sort of "plump" the thread.

Perle cotton is another type of cotton thread. It comes in different thicknesses and has been tightly twisted, giving a heavier, more textured look. For most of these projects, I've used floss and perle cotton manufactured by the DMC Corporation because it is inexpensive and widely available; numbers indicate specific colors.

There are also several manufacturers of hand-overdyed variegated floss (see Resources, page 155), and these lovely threads can be used to achieve gorgeous effects. Dyed in sections, so that the color of the thread changes automatically as you embroider, these flosses are expensive and available from a limited number of retailers, but are well worth it for certain projects. I've included their use in a couple of the ones I've designed here.

Needles

For decorative embroidery, a "crewel" needle—the kind with a nice, sharp point and a fairly large eye—is what you want, though its size will depend on the size of your thread, the size of your fingers, the tightness or looseness of your fabric, and your personal preference. Generally, you want a needle that is large enough to hold your thread without fraying it, but not so large that it leaves a hole in your fabric as it passes through. Crewel needles are numbered 1 through 10; 1 is the largest, 10 the smallest. Most are sold in small packages that include several sizes. It is worth having a good selection on hand, and experimenting with several until you find the size and quality that work for you and your projects. I almost always find myself happiest with a size 6 crewel needle for decorative embroidery—you'll probably find that you're happy somewhere between 5 and 7, too.

Storybook Pillowcases

Deep down, I am a practical person: I love beautiful, framed pieces of embroidery, but my heart really belongs to items that combine the decorative with the functional. Pillowcases are my favorite representatives from that industrious group of domestic beauties that are both gorgeous *and* used—*really* used—every day. Available in almost any color you could want, pillowcases made of high-thread-count cotton (and now even bamboo, which, I must say, feels fantastic and irons beautifully) are readily available. Embroidering on them is a pleasure, since placing the design so close to the edge of the case means you won't be dragging your hand back and forth under lots of fabric. ✂ Inspired by a traditional Hungarian design, this charming heart-and-flowers arrangement reminds me of something you might see decorating Goldilocks's pillow. I think it's just right.

Skill Level
EMBROIDERY: Medium
FINISHING: Easy

Finished Size
Fits the border of a standard- or king-size pillowcase

Materials
• TEMPLATE
  Storybook Pillowcases template (page 26)

• FABRIC
  One pair of ready-made pillowcases

• EMBROIDERY THREAD
  DMC cotton 6-strand embroidery floss

• CLEAR PLASTIC RULER

• CREWEL NEEDLE

• 4" (10CM) EMBROIDERY HOOP

Thread Guide

COLOR NUMBER		COLOR
666	■	Christmas Red, bright
935	■	Avocado Green, dark
733	■	Olive Green, medium
761	■	Salmon, light
893	■	Carnation, light
798	■	Delft Blue, dark
799	■	Delft Blue, medium

Prepare the pillowcases and transfer the design

Wash and dry the pillowcases on a normal cycle and press them smooth. Copy the template, enlarging it 137%, and cut the design from the paper, leaving a ¼" (6mm) margin. Select a transfer technique (see Transferring Designs, page 16) and transfer the design to the pillowcase, centering it both vertically and horizontally on the hem of the pillowcase. Repeat for the second pillowcase.

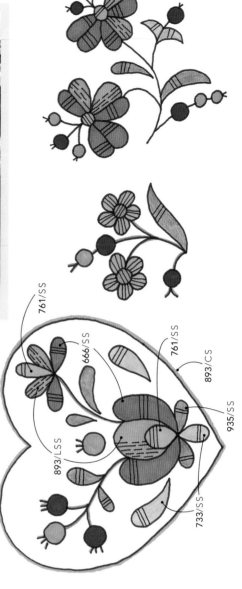

Embroider the design

Stitch the project, following the colors and stitches indicated in the diagram.

Finish the design

Refer to Finishing (page 154) to clean and press the pillowcases.

Storybook Pillowcases Template
Use 2 strands of floss throughout.
See page 14 for stitch abbreviations.
Enlarge template by 137%.

Thread Guide

COLOR NUMBER	COLOR	
666	■	Christmas Red, bright
935	■	Avocado Green, dark
733	■	Olive Green, medium
761	■	Salmon, light
893	■	Carnation, light
798	■	Delft Blue, dark
799	■	Delft Blue, medium

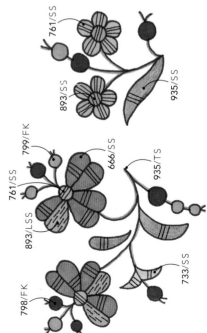

Apple Blossom Kerchief

Won't you look simply fetching in this little headscarf? I love cotton kerchiefs in the spring and summer—they're as protective as hats, but more charming and old-fashioned, somehow. A corner motif is perfectly at home. The embroidery goes very quickly, as most of it is done in backstitch. If you can handle a little finishing, this is a good starter project for beginners, and would make a lovely springtime gift for a sister or best friend. Or keep it for yourself, and consider growing your hair out so you can put it in two braids to peek out from under your summer kerchief.

✦ ✦

Skill Level
EMBROIDERY: Easy
FINISHING: Medium

Finished Size
16" x 16" (40.5cm x 40.5cm) with 14" (35.5cm) ties

Materials
- TEMPLATE
  Apple Blossom Kerchief template (page 28)

- FABRIC
  ½ yd (45.5cm) of 45"- (114cm-) wide cotton
- EMBROIDERY THREAD
  DMC cotton 6-strand embroidery floss
- 2½ YD (229CM) OF ¼"- (6MM-) WIDE (WHEN FOLDED) DOUBLE-FOLD BIAS TAPE
- CREWEL NEEDLE

- 4" (10CM) EMBROIDERY HOOP
- STRAIGHT PINS
- CLEAR PLASTIC RULER
- ROTARY CUTTER
- SELF-HEALING CUTTING MAT
- SEWING THREAD MATCHED TO THE COLOR OF THE BIAS TAPE
- SEWING MACHINE

Thread Guide

COLOR NUMBER		COLOR
605	▨	Cranberry, very light
961	◼	Dusty Rose, dark
818	☐	Baby Pink
564	▨	Jade, very light
3013	▨	Khaki Green, light
745	☐	Yellow, light pale
938	■	Coffee Brown, ultra dark
352	▨	Coral, light

✦ ✦

Prepare the fabric and transfer the design

1. Cut the fabric into 2 right triangles, with the short sides measuring 16" (40.5cm), and the long (diagonal) side measuring about 22 ½" (57cm).

2. Copy the template, enlarging it 123%, and cut the design from the paper, leaving a ¼" (6mm) margin. Select a transfer technique (see Transferring Designs, page 16) and transfer the design to the kerchief, leaving about 1" (2.5cm) margin between the edges of the kerchief and the design.

Embroider the design

Stitch the project, following the colors and stitches indicated in the diagram.

Finish the kerchief

1. Refer to Finishing (page 154) to clean and press the embroidery. With the wrong sides facing, pin the triangles together. Baste around all of the edges, a scant ¼" (6mm) from the edge. Trim the seams close to the stitching.

2. Apply the bias tape binding by machine along the short edges of the triangle (this should use up about 1 yard [91cm]): With the right side of the tape facing the back side of the kerchief, match the raw edge of the unfolded tape to the raw edge of the fabric, and pin along the fold line. Stitch along the fold line, and trim the resulting seam slightly. Fold the binding over the edge of the kerchief (to the right side), enclosing the raw edges, and pin the folded edge of the binding smoothly. Carefully machine-stitch the binding to the kerchief through all layers, keeping the seam close to the folded edge of the binding.

3. Find the center of the remaining length of the bias tape binding. Matching the center of the binding with the center of the long edge of the triangle, pin the binding as you did for the short edges, along the long edge of the triangle with the ends of the binding hanging off of either end. (These will be the ties.) Fold in the short ends ½" (13mm); fold the binding over the edge of the kerchief and pin the ends to hold the hems in place. With the kerchief right side up, beginning at the left end of the long tie, machine-stitch through all layers neatly down the length of the tie, across the kerchief edge, and down the other length of the tie, backstitching at each end to secure.

Thread Guide

COLOR NUMBER		COLOR
605		Cranberry, very light
961		Dusty Rose, dark
818		Baby Pink
564*		Jade, very light
3013*		Khaki Green, light
745		Yellow, light pale
938		Coffee Brown, ultra dark
352		Coral, light

Apple Blossom Kerchief template

Use 2 strands of floss throughout unless indicated by *; then use 1. See page 14 for stitch abbreviations. Enlarge template by 123%.

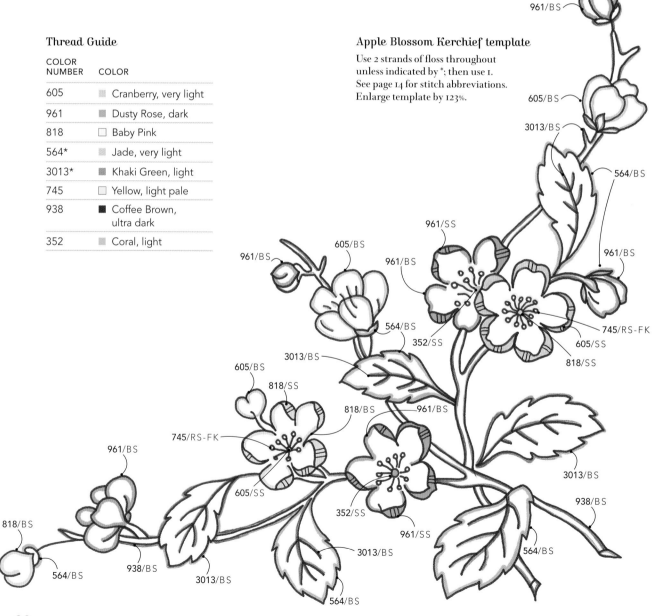

Country Time Quilt

A flock of friendly farm animals decorates this simple patchwork quilt, perfect for the animal-loving little one in your life. Six special patches—embroidered before they are sewn into the strips—are stitched almost in chain stitch, which makes a substantial yet delicate outline. ✂ As far as quilts go, random patches are the perfect stash-buster—you can literally use up to thirty different scraps you have lying around after finishing other projects. Choose fabrics that have a light, springtime feel— polka dots, ginghams, and tiny calicos are farm-fresh choices. I omitted the binding on purpose here, so this is a simple stitch-and-turn model; I didn't want anything interfering with those embroidered squares.

Skill Level

EMBROIDERY: Medium

FINISHING: Medium

Finished Size

37½" x 37½" (95cm x 95cm)

Materials

- TEMPLATE
  Country Time Quilt template
  (pages 34–35)

- FABRIC
  For embroidered patches:
  Six 12" x 12" (30.5cm x 30.5cm)
  squares of white cotton

  For quilt top: Thirty 7" x 7" (18cm
  x 18cm) squares of assorted cotton
  calicos, polka dots, and ginghams

  For quilt back: 1¼ yd (114cm) of
  45"- (114cm-) wide cotton

  For batting: 1¼ yd (114cm) of
  45"- (114cm-) wide cotton batting

- EMBROIDERY THREAD
  DMC cotton 6-strand
  embroidery floss
- CREWEL NEEDLE
- 4" (10CM) EMBROIDERY HOOP
- DRESSMAKER'S CHALK
- CLEAR PLASTIC RULER
- ROTARY CUTTER
- SELF-HEALING CUTTING MAT
- 36 MEDIUM-SIZED SAFETY PINS
- STRAIGHT PINS
- SEWING THREAD MATCHED TO THE
  COLOR OF THE FABRIC
- SEWING MACHINE

Thread Guide

COLOR NUMBER	COLOR
353	Peach
603	Cranberry
225	Shell Pink, ultra very light
Ecru	Ecru
310	Black
414	Steel Gray, dark
838	Beige Brown, very dark
413	Pewter Gray, dark
733	Olive Green, medium
906	Parrot Green, medium
3772	Desert Sand, very dark
3773	Desert Sand, medium
3045	Yellow Beige, dark
434	Brown, light
817	Coral Red, very dark
3854	Autumn Gold, medium
3855	Autumn Gold, light
3823	Yellow, ultra pale
996	Electric Blue, medium
598	Turquoise, light

Prepare the fabric and transfer the designs

1. Wash and dry the fabric on a normal cycle and press it smooth. For each white square, with dressmaker's chalk, mark a 7" (18cm) square centered inside each extra margin around the smaller square will help when hooping the fabric to embroider.

2. Copy the template, enlarging it 145%, and cut the design from the paper, leaving a ¼" (6mm) margin. Select a transfer technique (see Transferring Designs, page 16) and transfer the design to the square. Repeat for each of the 6 designs.

Embroider the designs

Stitch the patches, following the colors and stitches indicated in the diagram.

Finish the embroidered patches

Refer to Finishing (page 154) to clean and press the patches. After pressing, cut away the extra fabric around the marked 7" (18cm) square.

Make the quilt top

1. Lay out all of the squares on a flat surface, arranging the embroidered pieces so that they are spaced evenly—1 embroidered piece per row and 1 per column. With the right sides of the squares together,

using a ¼" (6mm) seam, stitch each row of squares into a strip of 6 patches. Press all seams on the prints open, and press the seams around the embroidered patches toward the prints (so the seams don't show through to the front of the embroidered patch).

2. Lay out the 6 strips, right side up and parallel. Starting at one end, pin (with straight pins) 2 strips together, right sides facing and seams matching. Stitch down the length using a ¼" (6mm) seam. Repeat for each strip, adding a new strip to the ever-growing quilt top, one after another. Press all seams away from embroidered patches, clipping if necessary.

Finish the quilt

1. To make the quilt "sandwich," lay the batting on a flat surface. Lay the backing piece right side up on top of the batting. Lay the quilt top right side down, on top of the backing. (The quilt top will be smaller than the batting and the quilt back piece.) Starting in the center of the quilt, pin a safety pin through the center of each square, pinning all 3 layers together smoothly. Pin around the edges of the quilt sandwich with straight pins.

2. Using a ¼" (6mm) seam, stitch all 3 layers of the quilt together around all 4 edges, pivoting at corners, and leaving a 6" (15cm) opening along the bottom edge. (You'll turn the quilt through this opening.) Trim the excess batting and backing, making sure all of your edges are smooth and straight. Trim corners and turn quilt right side out through opening.

3. Press around all edges. Turn in edges of opening and hand-stitch opening closed. Using 3 strands of embroidery floss in color 414 (Steel Gray, dark), make running stitches through all layers around all patches except the embroidered ones, keeping stitches ¼" (6mm) from seams.

Country Time Quilt template

Use 2 strands of floss throughout.
See page 14 for stitch abbreviations.
Enlarge template by 145%.

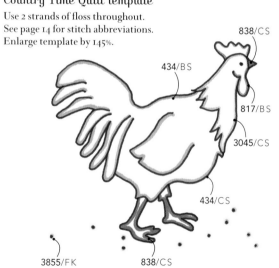

838/CS

434/BS

817/BS

3045/CS

434/CS

3855/FK   838/CS

310/SS

310/CS

310/BS

ECRU/CS

310/CS

603/SS

353/LD   603/SS

225/LD

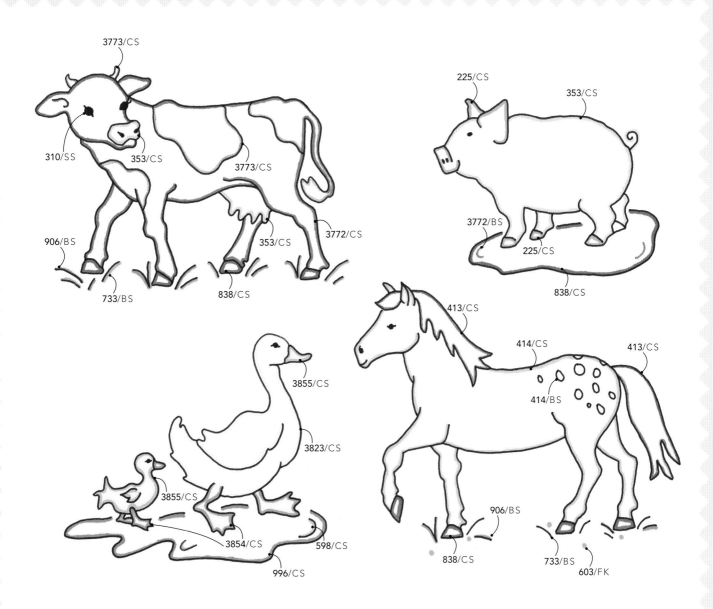

Thread Guide

COLOR NUMBER	COLOR		COLOR NUMBER	COLOR	
353	☐	Peach	3772	▦	Desert Sand, very dark
603	▦	Cranberry	3773	▦	Desert Sand, medium
225	▦	Shell Pink, ultra very light	3045	▦	Yellow Beige, dark
Ecru	▦	Ecru	434	▦	Brown, light
310	■	Black	817	▦	Coral Red, very dark
414	▦	Steel Gray, dark	3854	▦	Autumn Gold, medium
838	▦	Beige Brown, very dark	3855	▦	Autumn Gold, light
413	▦	Pewter Gray, dark	3823	☐	Yellow, ultra pale
733	▦	Olive Green, medium	996	▦	Electric Blue, medium
906	▦	Parrot Green, medium	598	▦	Turquoise, light

Dot-and-Daisy Café Curtains

Don't overlook the inherent potential in geometric-printed fabrics for decorative embroidery. Here, lazy daisies make use of evenly staggered polka dots for a crisp, cute border treatment—I used perle cotton #5, a satiny, twisted thread that reflects light beautifully and gives projects a dimensional quality that I like. To stitch the flowers, you'll carry the thread loosely across the back of the fabric from dot to dot, then snip it in between each flower and tie the ends into a knot. Though it's a little time consuming, this technique keeps the thread from showing through the fabric when light makes the back of your work more visible than you might desire.

Skill Level

EMBROIDERY: Easy
FINISHING: Medium

Finished Size of Each Curtain

Varies, determined by individual window

Materials

- FABRIC

For these curtains, I used decorator-weight cotton fabric with ½"- (13mm-) wide staggered polka dots and Wrights® Magic Curtain Tape #145-2007-001. To determine the length of each panel, measure the distance between your curtain rod and the windowsill, then add 8" (20cm) to the top for the top hem, and another 3" (7.5cm) to the bottom for a bottom hem. If you're planning to use 2 panels per window, the width of each unfinished panel should be equal to 2½ times the gathered width of each finished curtain. The amount of curtain tape you need will be equal to the width of each unfinished panel. In other words, if you want the gathered, finished curtain to be 12" (30cm) wide, your panel will be 30" (76cm), and you will need 30" (76cm) of Magic Curtain Tape. BE SURE that when you cut your panels you are keeping the fabric pattern parallel to the edges, otherwise your border will be crooked! Take your window measurements to the fabric store, and they will help you determine how much yardage to purchase.

- EMBROIDERY THREAD
  DMC Perle Cotton #5
- WRIGHTS® MAGIC CURTAIN TAPE #145-2007-001 (see "Fabric" for directions on determining amount)
- CREWEL NEEDLE
- 4" (10cm) EMBROIDERY HOOP
- SEWING THREAD MATCHED TO THE COLOR OF THE FABRIC
- SEWING MACHINE
- CLIP-ON CURTAIN RINGS (quantity depends on how wide your panel is; place 1 ring at every set of pleats)

Thread Guide

COLOR NUMBER		COLOR
666	■	Christmas Red, bright
352	■	Coral, light

Prepare the fabric

Wash and dry the fabric on a normal cycle, removing fabric from dryer while it is still damp. Press it smooth and cut it into individual panels.

Make the panels

1. Since the hems of the curtains do not interfere with the embroidery, you can finish the curtains before embroidering them. First, hem each long side edge: Turn under the edge ½" (13mm) and press; repeat the

4. On the first end of the tape, knot all 3 cords together. To gather the panel, begin to pull the cords from the other side until the panel is pleated evenly. Knot the cords securely, close to the last pleat. Hide the excess cord behind the finished panel so that you can release the knots later when it's time to wash the curtains, but do not cut the cord.

5. To hem the bottom edge, fold under 1½" (3.8cm) and press, repeat the procedure, and pin. By hand, tack the hem to the wrong side of the panel using hemstitch (see Illustrated Stitch Guide, page 146).

Embroider the design

1. The flowers on this curtain are made of 4 lazy daisy stitches whose petals are at right angles to each other with a contrast color French knot in the center of the petals. Using 1 strand of thread begin your embroidery on the first full row of dots above the turned-up hem. Work 4 lazy daisy stitches to create each flower, and repeat across an entire row, carrying thread loosely across the back of the panel as you work each daisy. Don't worry about the centers yet. Repeat until you have 4 rows of daisies, alternating between red and coral.

2. When all of the flowers have been stitched, turn the panel over and, one by one, snip the threads between flowers and tie the ends into a knot behind each flower, being careful not to pucker the embroidery on the front by pulling too tightly. Snip off the long ends of thread.

procedure, then machine-stitch, close to edge. On the top edge press under 4" (10cm), and then fold down 4" (10cm) again and press to make a double hem. Machine-stitch close to bottom edge of the hem.

2. Lay the Wrights® Magic Curtain Tape on the work surface with the pastel line facing you and at the top of tape. Pull the strings out of the tape 2" (5cm). Cut the tape ½" (13mm) from the strings and fold the end under.

3. Pin the folded end of tape even with the side hem of the panel. Align the long edge of the tape with the folded top edge of the panel and pin it in place. Fold the second end of the tape under and pin it close to the side hem. Stitch the tape to the panel along the top edge, the bottom edge, and between the draw cords, being careful not to catch the draw cords in your stitching.

3. Make French knots in contrasting color for each flower along each row. Turn panel over, and snip and tie each knot in place as you did for the flowers.

Finish the embroidery

Refer to Finishing (page 154) to clean and press the embroidery.

Notions Needle Book

Once you become hooked on embroidery, you'll need a place to keep your needles and pins. Don't do what I do, and stick them in the backrest of the sofa. Put them in this little felt folder, which encloses four "pages" of felt to hold your sharps. Finished with a running-stitch border and pinked edge, the simple sewing here means that once the embroidery is done you're almost good to go. Consider making a few more for stitching friends: No one can resist cute notions. It's impossible.

Skill Level
EMBROIDERY: Easy
FINISHING: Easy

Finished Size
3⅝" x 5½" (9cm x 14cm)

Materials
- TEMPLATE
  Notions Needle Book template and Tab Template (page 40)

- FABRIC
  For cover: One 7¼" x 5½" (18.5cm x 14cm) piece of wool or wool-blend felt

  For tab: One 3" x 3" (7.5cm x 7.5cm) piece of wool or wool-blend felt

For pages: Two 6½" x 5" (16.5cm x 12.5cm) pieces of cream wool or wool-blend felt

- EMBROIDERY THREAD
  DMC cotton 6-strand embroidery floss
- CREWEL NEEDLE
- CLEAR PLASTIC RULER
- ROTARY CUTTER
- SELF-HEALING CUTTING MAT
- PINKING SHEARS
- SMALL BUTTON
- SEWING THREAD MATCHED TO THE COLOR OF THE FABRIC
- SEWING MACHINE

Thread Guide

COLOR NUMBER		COLOR
321	■	Christmas Red, dark
913	■	Nile Green, medium
E415	■	Metallic Silver
743	■	Yellow, medium
E3821	■	Metallic Gold
824	■	Blue, very dark
996	■	Electric Blue, medium
3787	■	Brown Gray, dark
603	■	Cranberry
3023	■	Brown Gray, light
Blanc	□	White

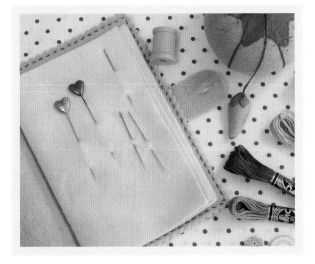

Transfer the designs and embroider

Make one copy of the Notions Needle Book template at 160% and cut each element out, leaving a ¼" (6mm) margin around each. Arrange elements as desired and transfer outlines to felt cover using an iron-on transfer pencil or dressmaker's chalk carbon paper (see Transferring Designs, page 16). Stitch the project, following the colors and stitches indicated in the diagram. Refer to Finishing (page 154) to clean and press the cover.

Finish the needle book

1. Trace (at 100%) and cut the tab used to close the needle book from a small scrap of felt, making a slit the width of your button with your embroidery scissors for the buttonhole. Trim the short, straight edge of the tab with pinking shears. Center the tab vertically on the left edge of the cover front and baste the pieces together.

2. Machine-stitch with thread matching the felt color along the outline of the needle book and on top of the tab. This will help reinforce the edges and secure the tab.

3. Cut out the needle book front just outside of the stitched border with pinking shears, turning the corners neatly. (It helps to practice on a few corners before you cut into your actual cover.) Lay the book with its right side down on a flat surface and center the pages vertically and horizontally on the felt. Pin them in place to hold, and machine-sew a seam down the center, through all layers and backstitching at each end, to create the spine.

4. Stitch the button to the front cover.

5. Using 2 strands of color 321 (Christmas Red, dark), make small running stitches on top of the line of machine stitching to decorate.

Notions Needle Book template

Use 2 strands of floss throughout, but use 1 strand gold and 1 strand silver on needle.
See page 14 for stitch abbreviations.
Enlarge template by 160%.

Thread Guide

COLOR NUMBER		COLOR
321	■	Christmas Red, dark
913	▥	Nile Green, medium
E415	▦	Metallic Silver
743	▢	Yellow, medium
E3821	▦	Metallic Gold
824	■	Blue, very dark
996	▦	Electric Blue, medium
3787	■	Brown Gray, dark
603	▦	Cranberry
3023	▦	Brown Gray, light
Blanc	☐	White

Tab template

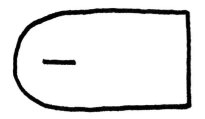

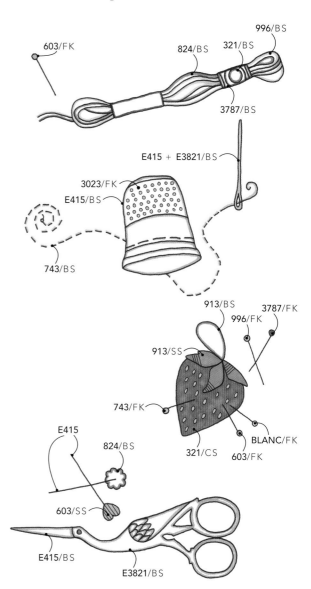

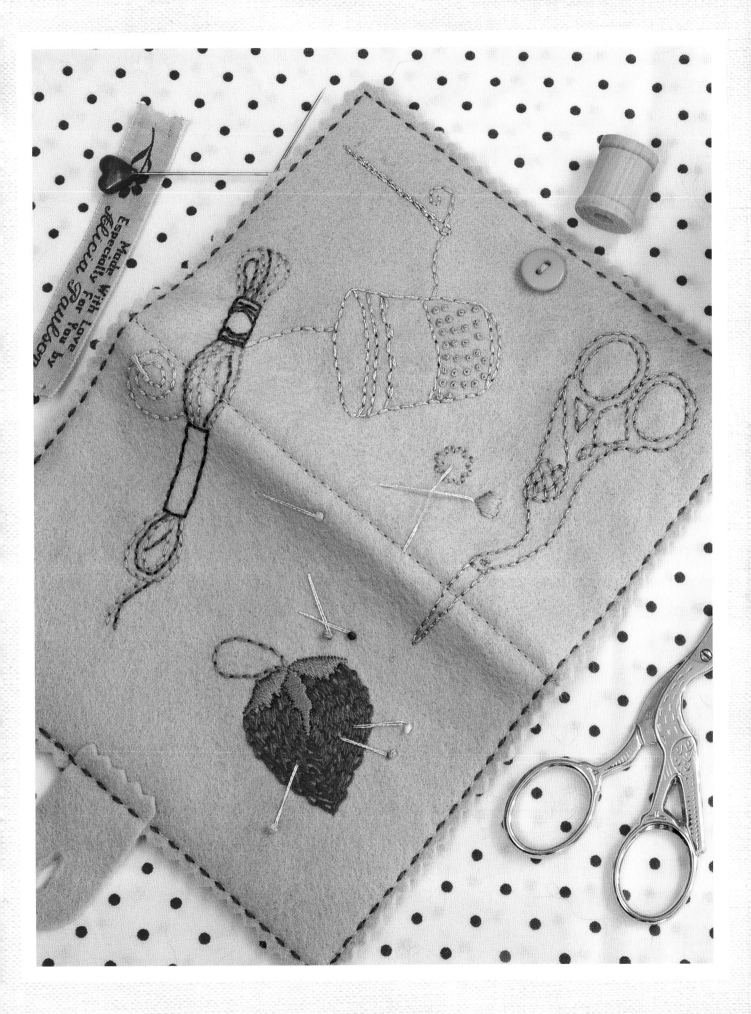

Strawberry Tablecloth

There's something so essentially satisfying about cooking and eating food you've grown or picked yourself. Weekends in June here in Oregon, when the strawberries are at their peak, we like to go out to our favorite farm and wander through the long rows of ruby fruit all morning, snapping stems as we go. They just taste better when you've squatted to gather them, somehow. ✄ Strawberries are also intensely picturesque! How sweet is this sprig of blossoms and berries, stitched in cotton floss on linen. Purchase some linen yardage at a fabric store and make the tablecloth any size you want, finishing the borders with a simple running stitch and fringed edge, or better yet stitch the design on a plain tablecloth already in your linen closet (or find one at Goodwill—there are tons). Summer mornings at the breakfast table were never prettier.

Skill Level
EMBROIDERY: Medium
FINISHING: Medium

Finished Size
Varies, depending on your table

Materials
- TEMPLATE
  Strawberry Tablecloth template (page 44)
- FABRIC
  A ready-made tablecloth, or linen yardage cut to any length desired. Make sure the fabric is wide enough after shrinkage—linen *will* shrink when washed—so that the edges of the finished tablecloth hang over the edge of the table about 6 inches (15cm) on all sides (any longer and the corner designs won't show up as well). If 54"- (137cm-) wide fabric (the typical width of linen sold by the yard) won't do it, you'll need to seam 2 lengths together to get the width your table needs.
  Note: Extra fabric can be cut up and made into napkins.
- EMBROIDERY THREAD
  DMC cotton 6-strand embroidery floss
- CLEAR PLASTIC RULER
- CREWEL NEEDLE
- 4" (10CM) EMBROIDERY-HOOP
- AIR-ERASE FABRIC MARKER OR DRESSMAKER'S CHALK
- SEWING THREAD MATCHED TO THE COLOR OF THE FABRIC
- SEWING MACHINE

Thread Guide

COLOR NUMBER		COLOR
934		Black Avocado Green
3011		Khaki Green, dark
469		Avocado Green
3855		Autumn Gold, light
321		Christmas Red
666		Christmas Red, bright
498		Christmas Red, dark
4160		White and Pink

Prepare the fabric

1. Wash and dry the fabric on a normal cycle, then press (don't go crazy here–wrinkles are in linen's nature, but pulling the fabric out of the dryer when it is still damp can help you press). Cut the fabric to the exact size you want your tablecloth to be. Try to cut the edges of the cloth on the grain of the fabric as much as possible; when you fringe the hem later (by pulling individual threads from the weave of the fabric), you'll thank yourself for fussing here.

2. Using thread the same color as your cloth, machine-sew around all of the edges of the cloth, 1" (2.5cm) from the raw edge, pivoting at the corners. Repeat, machine-sewing around the entire edge of the cloth again, halfway between the first row of

the stitching and the raw edge of the fabric. The top row of stitches, will guide your decorative running stitches, and the bottom row of stitches will prevent the frayed edges from fraying too high up the cloth.

Transfer the design

Copy the template, enlarging it 161%, and cut the design from the paper, leaving a ¼" (6mm) margin. In each corner of the fabric, measure and mark a point 3" (7.5cm) from each raw edge to help guide the placement of the design. Select a transfer technique (see Transferring Designs, page 16) and transfer the design to the tablecloth to align with the marks you just made.

Embroider the design

Stitch the project, following the colors and stitches indicated in the diagram.

Finish the tablecloth

Refer to Finishing (page 154) to clean and press the project. Using 6 strands of color 666 (Christmas red, bright) make running stitches around the entire edge of the cloth, following the inner, machine-sewn line of stitching you created in the first step. To fringe the edges, pull individual threads from each edge up to the outer line of stitching.

Strawberry Tablecloth template
Use 3 strands of floss to outline all stems and leaves; otherwise use 2 throughout. See page 14 for stitch abbreviations. Enlarge template by 161%.

Thread Guide

COLOR NUMBER		COLOR
934	■	Black Avocado Green
3011	■	Khaki Green, dark
469	■	Avocado Green
3855	■	Autumn Gold, light
321	■	Christmas Red
666	■	Christmas Red, bright
498	■	Christmas Red, dark
4160	■	White and Pink

Chicken Scratch Shelf Edging

Chicken scratch embroidery, also more prettily known as snowflaking, Amish lace, or Depression lace, is a type of early American embroidery made popular with housewives of the '30s and '40s who used this simple-but-lovely technique to decorate gingham aprons and sundresses. The careful placement of double cross-stitches and woven circle stitches on the white and colored squares of gingham gives the impression of appliquéd lace. Countless arrangements of these stitches can result in fantastic swaths of lacy borders. What difficulty my simple shelf-edging lacks in technique it makes up for in the potential tedium of repeating the same motif: To make six edgings for all of the shelves of my china cabinet required me to repeat the lacy diamond a wrist-twitching fifty-four times. (The number and width of your shelves will determine how many you need to make.) But the end result is so charming and delicate that the thought of your cake plates and teacups being shown to great effect on your newly snowflaked shelves will pull you through—I promise.

Skill Level
EMBROIDERY: Easy
FINISHING: Easy

Finished Size
Determined by the size of your individual shelf

Materials
- TEMPLATE
  Chicken Scratch Shelf Edging template (page 47)

- FABRIC
  For each shelf: One piece of ¼" (6mm) gingham measuring 4 squares wider and 25 squares deeper than your shelf (See directions for tips on cutting fabric)

- EMBROIDERY THREAD
  DMC cotton 6-strand embroidery floss

- CREWEL NEEDLE
- 4" (10CM) EMBROIDERY HOOP
- AIR-ERASE FABRIC MARKER OR DRESSMAKER'S CHALK
- SEWING THREAD MATCHED TO THE COLOR OF THE FABRIC
- SEWING MACHINE

Thread Guide

COLOR NUMBER	COLOR
Blanc	■ White

Note: White thread is shown as black on the template.

Cut the fabric

1. Measure the width and depth of your shelf and mark these dimensions on a piece of gingham using dressmaker's chalk or a fabric marker. Add 4 squares of gingham to the width, and mark. Add 25 squares to the depth, and mark. Your first and last columns of gingham should include white squares; your last row of gingham should include only colored squares (no white). If necessary, the fabric can be cut slightly smaller to accommodate. Fiddling with these measurements now will result in your embroidery being centered and even on the finished edging, so take your time here. Measure twice, cut once! Repeat this process for each piece of edging you need to cut.

2. To find the center gingham square of the bottom border, fold the fabric in half widthwise to find the center column; then, along this fold, count 18 rows up from the bottom edge. With the marker or chalk, mark this spot as the center square of the center motif.

Embroider the design

Using 2 strands of floss, stitch the project, following the colors and stitches indicated in the diagram. You don't need to transfer any stitch marks to the fabric; just consult the template to see where to make each straight stitch. Start with the center motif. Position the next motif 1 square from the edge of the first. You do not need to start embroidering at the center of the subsequent motifs; just start at the bottom corner closest to the motif you've already worked. Continue until you have stitched 4 motifs (or however many you need for the width of your shelf) on either side of the center motif.

Finish the edging

1. Refer to Finishing (page 154) to clean and press the edging.

2. Hem the long side edge: Turn under the edge ¼" (6mm) and press, repeat the procedure, then machine-stitch, close to edge. Along the top edge of the piece, turn under ¼" (6mm) and press, repeat the procedure, then machine-stitch, close to edge.

3. On the bottom edge (near the embroidery) press under ¼" (6mm), and then fold exactly 11 more squares up to the back side of the edging and pin. By hand, tack the hem to the wrong side of the edging using hemstitch (see Illustrated Stitch Guide, page 146). Press bottom fold well to create a sharp edge.

Chicken Scratch Shelf Edging template

Use 2 strands of floss throughout.

Thread Guide

COLOR NUMBER	COLOR
Blanc	■ White

Note: White thread is shown as black on the template.

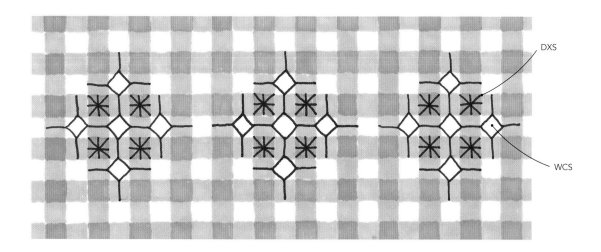

Days of the Week Dishtowels

In the late nineteenth century, simple outline embroidery done with colorfast "Turkey Red" thread was very popular. Penny squares—squares of muslin with printed images of flowers, fruits and vegetables, animals, household items, or historical figures that cost (you guessed it) one penny—were frequently given to young girls to practice their needlework, along with a skein of red floss. But even after advancements in dyeing made other colors reliable, "redwork," as all embroidery of this type came to be known, continued to be practiced, and still looks fresh and delightful as ever today. Here I've combined it with my own tongue-in-cheek take on another embroidered classic, the days-of-the-week dishtowels. My versions of the traditionally prescribed activities (Monday, wash day; Tuesday, ironing day; Wednesday, sewing day; Thursday, market day; Friday, cleaning day; Saturday, baking day; and finally Sunday, the day of rest) are updated to reflect my own domestic details.

Skill Level
EMBROIDERY: Easy
FINISHING: Easy

Finished Size
7 towels, each 16" (40.5cm) x 22" (56cm)

Materials
- TEMPLATE
  Days of the Week Dishtowels template (pages 50–51)

- FABRIC
  4⅔ yds (4.3m) of 16"- (40.5cm-) wide toweling with finished side edges (I used toweling made by Moda, in style #920, color 82 [Red] and 22 [Blueberry].)

- EMBROIDERY THREAD
  DMC cotton 6-strand embroidery floss

- CLEAR PLASTIC RULER
- ROTARY CUTTER
- SELF-HEALING CUTTING MAT
- CREWEL NEEDLE
- 4" (10CM) EMBROIDERY HOOP
- SEWING THREAD MATCHED TO THE COLOR OF THE FABRIC
- SEWING MACHINE

Thread Guide

COLOR NUMBER		COLOR
321	■	Christmas Red

Note: In order to show the templates clearly, red thread is shown as black on the template.

Prepare the towels and transfer the designs

Wash and dry the toweling on a normal cycle and press it smooth. Cut it into 7 equal lengths, 24" (61cm) each. Hem the top and bottom edges: turn under each edge ½" (13mm) and press, repeat the procedure, then machine-stitch close to the edge. Repeat for each towel. Copy the template, enlarging it 161%, and cut the designs from the paper, leaving a ¼" (6mm) margin. Select a transfer technique (see Transferring Designs, page 16) and transfer one design to each of the seven pieces of fabric.

Embroider the design

Stitch the entire design, including text, in backstitch. Repeat for each towel. Refer to Finishing (page 154) to clean and press the embroidery. Repeat for each towel. Refer to Finishing (page 154) to clean and press the embroidery.

Days of the Week Dishtowels template

Use 2 strands of floss throughout.
Enlarge template by 161%.

Thread Guide

COLOR NUMBER	COLOR
321	■ Christmas Red

Note: In order to show the templates clearly, red thread is shown as black on the template.

Monday

Tuesday

Wednesday

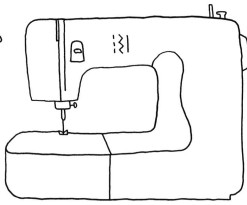

Thursday

Friday

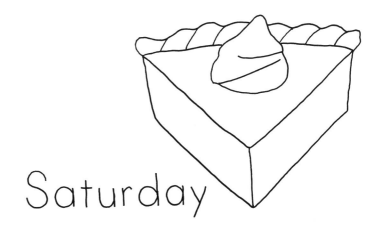

Saturday

Sunday

Plum Tree Tablecloth

Outside my window today, the plum tree in our front yard is in bloom. In fact, we have one in the backyard as well; our neighbors have one and our other neighbors have three—so outside almost every window in our house in early April there is a froth of lavender. Later this week the trees will start dropping fairyland petals, and later this summer the branches will be filled with plums, their hazy purple skins hiding ruby-red flesh. I love that color combination. This tablecloth makes up quickly. Its simple repeat is made of straight stitches that rely on the weave of the fabric to provide a grid—no pattern transferring necessary. And with no changes of color to fuss with, you'll likely be done before the blossoms outside are.

❖ ❖

Skill Level
EMBROIDERY: Easy
FINISHING: Easy

Finished Size
Varies, depending on your table

Materials
- TEMPLATE
  Plum Tree Tablecloth template (page 54)

- FABRIC
  One piece of decorator-weight ½" (13mm) cotton gingham that is 20" (51cm) longer and 20" (51cm) wider than your table. (See directions for tips on cutting fabric.)

- EMBROIDERY THREAD
  DMC cotton 6-strand embroidery floss

- CREWEL NEEDLE

- 4" (10CM) EMBROIDERY HOOP

- AIR-ERASE FABRIC MARKER OR DRESSMAKER'S CHALK

- SEWING THREAD MATCHED TO THE COLOR OF THE FABRIC

- SEWING MACHINE

Thread Guide

COLOR NUMBER	COLOR
321	■ Christmas Red

Prepare the fabric and make the tablecloth

1. Wash and dry the fabric on a normal cycle and press it smooth.

2. To cut the fabric, first measure the width and length of your table. Mark these dimensions on the gingham using dressmaker's chalk or a fabric marker. Add 20 squares to each side and mark. Your first and last columns of gingham should include white squares; your last row of gingham should include only colored squares (no white). Fiddling with these measurements now will result in your embroidery being centered and even on the finished edging, so take your time here. When you've got it right, then cut the fabric.

   If your table is wide, you may need to purchase two lengths and seam the lengths to create the size tablecloth you need.

3. Hem each side edge: turn the edge under 1 row and press, repeat the procedure, then machine-stitch close to edge. (To miter the corners, see General Sewing Techniques, page 152.)

Embroider the design

1. Find the center gingham square of the bottom border: Fold the fabric in half widthwise to find the center column (it should include only colored squares); then, along this fold, count 5 rows up from the bottom edge. With the marker or chalk, mark this spot as the center square of the bottom-center diamond on the center motif.

2. Following the chart, embroider this center motif, diamond by diamond. Continue stitching the rest of the design in relation to this central motif, stopping at either (short) end when there are no longer enough squares to complete an entire motif.

Plum Tree Tablecloth template
Use 6 strands of floss throughout

Thread Guide

COLOR NUMBER	COLOR
321	■ Christmas Red

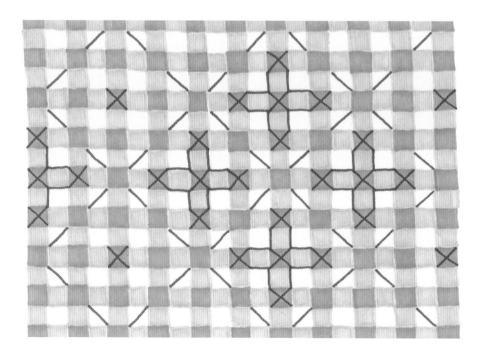

Petunia Headband

Headbands are so pretty and practical—my favorite combination in an accessory. With a minimum amount of fiddly finishing necessary, you are freed up to really concentrate on the embroidery itself. This design is inspired by a traditional Scandinavian tole border. I updated it in hot pink and orange on a mustard-colored background, perfect for a hazy summer night. Slip it on and find yourself an outdoor concert to attend!

Skill Level
EMBROIDERY: Medium
FINISHING: Medium

Finished Size
15" x 1½" (38cm x 3.8cm) not including elastic

Materials
- TEMPLATE
  Petunia Headband template (page 56)
- FABRIC
  One 17" x 9½" (43cm x 24cm) piece of cotton
- EMBROIDERY THREAD
  DMC cotton 6-strand embroidery floss
- ONE 8" (20.5CM) LENGTH OF DECORATIVE ELASTIC
- CREWEL NEEDLE
- 4" (10CM) EMBROIDERY HOOP
- CLEAR PLASTIC RULER
- ROTARY CUTTER
- SELF-HEALING CUTTING MAT
- LARGE SAFETY PIN
- SEWING THREAD MATCHED TO THE COLOR OF THE FABRIC
- SEWING MACHINE

Thread Guide

COLOR NUMBER		COLOR
935	■	Avocado Green, dark
164	■	Forest Green, light
350	■	Coral, medium
971	■	Pumpkin
3716	■	Dusty Rose, very light
602	■	Cranberry, medium
732	□	Olive Green

Prepare the fabric

Fold the piece of fabric in half lengthwise and then again widthwise to find its center. Using your clear plastic ruler and a Micron marker, draw a rectangle 16" (40.5cm) wide and 3½" (9cm) tall, using the center point of the fabric as the center point of the rectangle. You will cut the headband out along this outline when you are finished embroidering it, but for now, just leave the fabric intact—the extra fabric around the outline will allow you to hoop the design with ease.

Transfer the design

Copy the template, enlarging it 106%, and cut the design from the paper, leaving a ¼" (6mm) margin. Select a transfer technique (see Transferring Designs, page 16) and transfer the design to the fabric.

Embroider the design

Stitch the project, following the colors and stitches indicated in the diagram. Refer to Finishing (page 154) to clean and press the embroidery.

Petunia Headband template

Use 2 strands of floss throughout.
See page 14 for stitch abbreviations.
Enlarge template by 106%.

Thread Guide

COLOR NUMBER	COLOR
935	■ Avocado Green, dark
164	■ Forest Green, light
350	■ Coral, medium
971	■ Pumpkin
3716	■ Dusty Rose, very light
602	■ Cranberry, medium
732	□ Olive Green

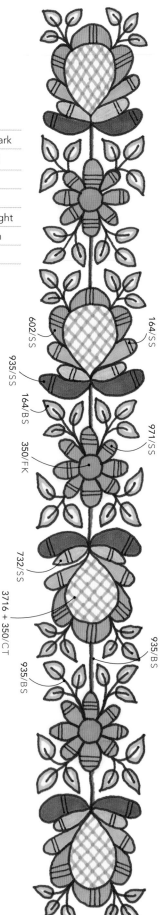

Finish the headband

1. Following the outline drawn earlier, cut the headband from the piece of fabric.

2. Fold the headband in half lengthwise, with the right sides together and the raw edges even. Using a ¼" (6mm) seam, machine-sew down the length of the headband. Attach the safety pin to one end of the headband; snake the safety pin inside the tube of fabric and pull it out the other end to turn the tube. Centering the embroidery on the front side of the tube, press the folded edges of the headband.

3. Fold each short end of the tube in ½" (13mm) and press. Insert one end of the piece of elastic into one end of the tube and baste to secure it temporarily. Place the headband on your head to determine how long the elastic that joins the ends of the headband should be; it should fit comfortably (this step is easier if you have a helper to hold the headband on for you, and mark the elastic's length). Remove the headband, trim the elastic ½" (13mm) beyond the marked length, and insert the elastic into the other end of the tube, basting to hold.

4. With a sharp needle, hand-stitch the ends of the headband closed using a whipstitch (see General Sewing Techniques, page 152) making sure to add a few extra stitches to secure the elastic in the ends of the tube.

Petal Pillowcases

Once used as a means of identifying the laundry of the upper class (so that your family's very nice white sheets didn't get mistaken for another family's not-so-nice white sheets when they were all sent out for washing), today's embroidered monograms enjoy more populist applications, and almost any catalogue that sells linens will machine-embroider yours for a few dollars. Resist the urge to order them, and instead spend a few peaceful hours perfecting your stitching with these fancy, springtime-evoking initials. In watercolored pinks and greens, each gorgeous letter and attendant blossoms are made of padded satin stitches, which give both the monogram and flowers a silky, dimensional look that subtly reflects light and lends a luscious, luxurious look. To embroider the second of the pair, be sure to position the pillowcase with its hem facing the opposite direction of the first, so that when the bed is made each pillow will show off its moniker perfectly.

Skill Level

EMBROIDERY: Difficult

FINISHING: Easy

Finished Size

Fits the border of a standard- or king-size pillowcase

Materials

- TEMPLATE

  Petal Pillowcases template (pages 61–63)

- FABRIC

  One pair of ready-made pillowcases

- EMBROIDERY THREAD

  DMC cotton 6-strand embroidery floss

- CLEAR PLASTIC RULER

- CREWEL NEEDLE

- 4" (10CM) EMBROIDERY HOOP

Thread Guide

COLOR NUMBER		COLOR
603	■	Cranberry
3713	▨	Salmon, very light
926	▨	Gray Green, medium
372	▨	Mustard, light
833	▨	Golden Olive, light
3856	▨	Mahogany, ultra very light
3047	□	Yellow Beige, light

Prepare the pillowcases and transfer the design

Wash and dry the pillowcases on a normal cycle and press them smooth. Copy the template, enlarging it 222% (139% for the A), and cut the design from the paper, leaving a ¼" (6mm) margin. Transfer the design to the pillowcase (see Transferring Designs, page 16) centering it both vertically and horizontally on the hem of the pillowcase.

Embroider the design

Stitch the project, following the colors and stitches indicated in the diagram.

Finish the design

Refer to Finishing (page 154) to clean and press the pillowcases.

Petal Pillowcases template

Use 2 strands of floss throughout.
See page 14 for stitch abbreviations.
Enlarge "A" template by 139%;
 enlarge all others by 222%.

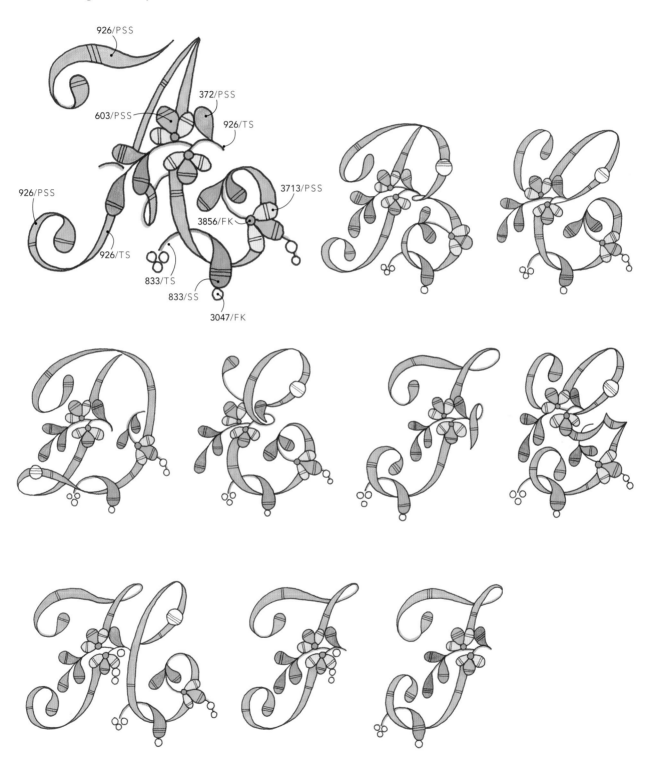

926/PSS
372/PSS
603/PSS
926/TS
926/PSS
3713/PSS
3856/FK
926/TS
833/TS
833/SS
3047/FK

Thread Guide

COLOR NUMBER		COLOR
603	■	Cranberry
3713	■	Salmon, very light
926	■	Gray Green, medium
372	■	Mustard, light
833	■	Golden Olive, light
3856	■	Mahogany, ultra very light
3047	■	Yellow Beige, light

Gretel Skirt

Alpine-inspired apparel seems *made* for embroidery, especially traditional, gathered dirndl-type skirts. This one has a separate overskirt that splits in front and a figure-flattering yoke you'll draft a pattern for from a straight, fitted skirt you already have in your closet. You'll need a knowledge of general apparel-sewing techniques here, including zipper installation, but there's nothing too complicated about this. Both bottom layers are simply made out of gathered, straight-sided panels; I chose this luscious baby-blue baby-wale corduroy because nothing gathers—or drapes—quite like this soft, scrumptious stuff. ✄ If you aren't feeling ambitious enough to sew the whole skirt, just add these pretty Ukrainian-inspired corner borders to any skirt with a defined center-front seam. Embroider the flowers after the skirt is finished, then dress up in this little beauty and invite some folks over for spiced cider and fondue.

Skill Level
EMBROIDERY: Difficult
FINISHING: Difficult

Finished Size
Varies depending on personal measurements

Seam allowance
½" (13mm)

Materials
• TEMPLATE
  Gretel Skirt template
  (page 67)

• FABRIC
  For skirt: 3 to 3½ yd (275cm to 320cm) of 45"- (114cm)-wide baby-wale corduroy, depending on the size and length of the skirt
  For trim: 3½ yd (320cm) of 1"- (2.5cm-) wide rickrack
  For lining yoke: ⅞ yd (80cm) of 22"- (56cm-) wide lightweight fusible interfacing

• EMBROIDERY THREAD
  DMC cotton 6-strand embroidery floss

• ONE 7" (18CM) ZIPPER

• LARGE PIECE OF NEWSPRINT, OR OTHER PAPER ON WHICH TO DRAFT THE SKIRT YOKE
• LEAD PENCIL
• TAPE MEASURE
• CLEAR PLASTIC RULER
• CREWEL NEEDLE
• 4" (10CM) EMBROIDERY HOOP
• SEWING THREAD MATCHED TO THE COLOR OF THE FABRIC
• SEWING MACHINE

Thread Guide

COLOR NUMBER		COLOR
666	■	Christmas Red, bright
742	■	Tangerine, light
3051	■	Green Gray, dark
353	■	Peach
760	■	Salmon
3347	■	Yellow Green, medium
3371	■	Black Brown

Make the yoke pattern and the yoke

1. Find a skirt in your closet with a dartless fitted waist. Place it on the newsprint and trace the waistline of the skirt with pencil, then continue 5" (12.5cm) down the length on each side.

2. Remove the skirt from the paper. Measure and mark a point 5" (12.5cm) below the center of the waistline.

Draw a line from this point across to the points you stopped at on each side seam, following the same curve as the waistline. Use your ruler to make sure your yoke is 5" (12.5cm) at the center front, 5" (12.5cm) at the side seam, and 5" (12.5cm) at each point along the curve. Mark the grainline parallel to the center front.

3. Add ½" (13mm) around all edges for the seam allowance. Cut out the pattern. From the pattern, cut 4 yoke pieces out of the corduroy fabric, and 2 yoke pieces out of interfacing. Trim a scant ½" (13mm) from around the edges of the interfacing pieces, and apply interfacing according to manufacturer's directions to the wrong sides of 2 yoke pieces; these are now the yoke front and the yoke back pieces. With the right sides together, stitch the yoke front to the back at the right side seam. With the right sides together, stitch the other yoke pieces together at the right side seam; this is now the yoke facing. Press all of the seams open. Press under ½" (13mm) on the bottom edge of the yoke facing and set yoke and yoke facing aside.

Make the underskirt

1. Determine how long you want your underskirt to be from waist to hem, and subtract 5" (12.5cm). Add 2½" (6.5cm) for the seam allowance and hem to this number—this is the length of your underskirt panels. Take your waist measurement and add 1" (2.5cm)—this is the width of each underskirt panel. For example: If you want the length of your finished skirt to be 25" (63.5cm) and your waist is 30" (76cm) around, your underskirt panel will be 31" x 22½" (79cm x 57cm). Write these measurements down; you'll use them again to calculate the dimensions of the overskirt. Cut 2 underskirt panels with these dimensions, keeping the length parallel to the grainline of the fabric.

2. With the right sides together, place a mark on the left side seam 2½" (6.5cm) from the top. Stitch the underskirt front to the back at side seams, leaving the seam open (for the zipper) above this mark.

3. Press up ½" (13mm) on the lower edge of the underskirt, then press up another 1½" (3.8cm) for the hem. Stitch the hem by hand with hemstitch (see General Sewing Techniques, page 152).

Make the overskirt

1. Using the final dimensions of the underskirt panels, subtract 3" (7.5cm) from the length and add 2" (5cm) to the width to determine the dimensions of the overskirt panels. Cut 2 skirt panels with these dimensions, keeping the length parallel to the grainline of the fabric, then trim 2" (5cm) from the width of one of the panels for the overskirt back. Fold the front panel in half widthwise, short ends together, and press the fold. Cut the panel in half along the fold—this will be the center opening.

2. With the right sides together, place a mark on the left side seam 2½" (6.5cm) from the top. Stitch the overskirt front to the overskirt back at the side seams, leaving the seam open above this mark. Clip the seam allowance to—but not through—the stitching at this mark.

3. Fold up ½" (13mm), press, and repeat to form a narrow hem around the bottom and the center front edges of the overskirt. Machine-stitch the hem in place. Pin the rickrack onto the wrong side of the overskirt around the bottom and the center front edges, leaving the scallops peeking out from the edges. Machine-stitch in place.

Gather the skirt and attach it to the yoke

1. Pin the wrong side of the overskirt to the right side of the underskirt, raw edges even, matching seams and overlapping the center front panels slightly at the center front of skirt. Bring the left side seam allowance to the inside above the clip. Baste the overskirt and the underskirt together around the left side seam opening and around the top edges. Gather the upper edges of the skirt to within 1" (2.5cm) of the left side seam openings.

2. With the right sides together, pin the bottom edge of the yoke to the top, gathered edge of the skirts,

matching the centers and side seam. Baste in place, then stitch the seam and press the seam allowance toward the yoke. Insert the zipper on the left side seam following the directions on the zipper package.

3. With the right sides together, pin the yoke facing to the skirt at the waistline. The facing will extend beyond the left side seam opening edges. Stitch the seam; trim the seam slightly and clip the curves. Turn the yoke facing to the inside, and press. Pin the pressed edge of the facing over the seam. Turn under and stitch the side edges to the zipper tape, and the lower edge over the seam by hand, using hemstitch (see General Sewing Techniques, page 152).

Embroider the design

1. Transfer the border design (it's at 100% here) to the corner edges of the overskirt, placing each edge of the design about 1 ½" (3.8cm) from each edge of the overskirt. Reverse the design for the left panel. (See Transferring Designs, page 16.)

2. Stitch the project, following the colors and stitches indicated in the diagram. Refer to Finishing (page 154) to clean and press the embroidery.

Gretel Skirt template
Use 2 strands of floss throughout.
See page 14 for stitch abbreviations.
Template is at 100%.

Thread Guide

COLOR NUMBER		COLOR
666	■	Christmas Red, bright
742	▦	Tangerine, light
3051	▨	Green Gray, dark
353	▨	Peach
760	▨	Salmon
3347	▨	Yellow Green, medium
3371	■	Black Brown

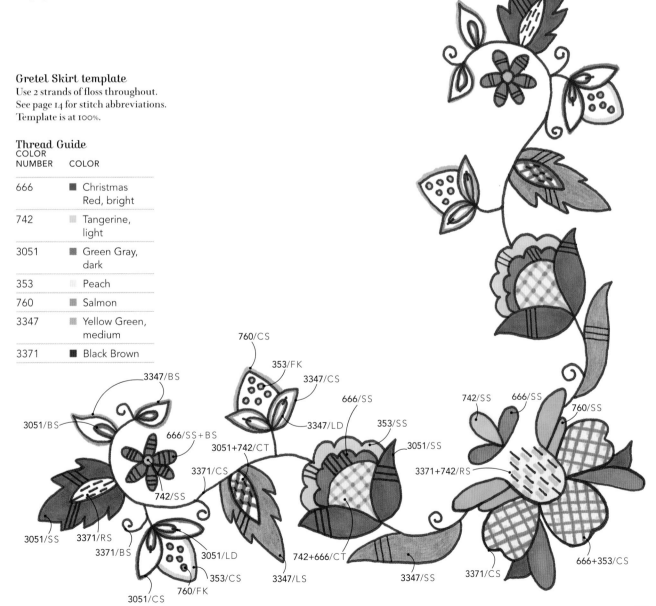

Counted

Cross

Stitch

Cross stitch has a long and industrious history, and is an important part of peasant craft and folk-art traditions from all over the world. As its name suggests, counted cross stitch embroidery uses groups of two straight stitches crossed at right angles and worked over a grid of perfect squares to create everything from simple motifs to complicated borders. The design is not printed onto the fabric, but done, stitch by stitch, while following a chart that indicates where to place each one, and in which color to work it. When looking at a cross-stitch chart, remember that each square on the chart represents one cross stitch on the fabric. And if the chart is too small to see comfortably, just make enlargements on a color copy machine.

Fabrics

Counted cross stitch is best done on evenweave fabric, which has an equal number of threads running both lengthwise (called the "warp") and crosswise (called the "weft"). The cross-stitched projects in this book are all done on evenweave linen, checked gingham, or on top of a special fabric called "waste canvas" (which provides a temporary and removable grid for use on virtually any type of fabric). Counted cross stitch can also be worked on a special cloth called Aida, the weave of which creates a very pronounced set of holes to guide your stitches (which can be helpful if you're just starting out). When it comes to fabric, the look and feel of a certain type of cloth, or the ease with which you are able to see the squares (!), is really a matter of personal preference.

What's more important is the "count" of the fabric. Cross-stitch fabrics are available in different counts. Stitch counts refer to the number of stitches you will get across the space, either vertically or horizontally, of 1 inch (2.5 centimeters). On a checked fabric like gingham, the count is easy to identify: Each colored (or white) square will hold one stitch, so ⅛" gingham has eight stitches per inch (2.5 centimeters), or (wait for it) a stitch count of eight. Waste canvas and Aida cloth have weaves which make the "squares" of the fabric obvious and easy to count (and the count is also listed on the packaging or the end of the bolt, if you're buying yardage). On evenweave linen, cross stitches are normally done over two threads in the fabric's weave, so cloth that has a thread count of twenty-eight threads per inch has a *stitch* count of fourteen.

Stitch count is of utmost importance when choosing fabrics for cross-stitching because designs look quite different when they are done on coarser-weave fabric, where the motifs will be bigger and the crosses more pronounced, or finer-weave fabric, where the motifs will be smaller and the individual crosses almost disappear. The directions for the projects in this book list the number of individual stitches in the design areas, as well as the stitch/thread count of the fabrics I chose, but you are certainly not limited to these. If you do decide to change the stitch count to another size, however, please note that *you must recalculate the size of the design*—divide the number of stitches in the design by the stitch count of your new fabric to get the height and width in inches of the new design area—and be sure to add three inches (7.5 centimeters) to each of the four sides so that you have enough extra fabric to work with when hooping or finishing.

As with decorative embroidery, if you're making something utilitarian, such as an apron (as opposed to a sampler, which is decorative), you'll want to prewash and dry your fabric on your regular cycle, or according to manufacturer's instructions.

Threads

Although cross stitch can be worked in cotton, wool, or silk thread, the projects in this book use either two or three strands of six-strand cotton floss (see Decorative Embroidery, page 20). The number of strands you use is, for the most part, dictated by the fabric thread count. If your fabric gets anywhere from eight to eleven stitches per inch (2.5 centimeters), use three strands of floss; between twelve to sixteen, use two strands, and on anything woven finer than sixteen threads per inch, use one strand.

Needles

Cross-stitching on evenweave fabric calls for large-eyed, blunt-tipped tapestry needles. These needles push through the weave of the fabric without piercing the warp or weft threads. They are sold in packages of assorted sizes, anywhere from size 20 to 28, and, as with crewel needles, it is worth testing out a few sizes until you find the one that works for you. It should be big enough to be held in place by the grid of the fabric without falling through, but small enough that it doesn't distort the threads significantly along the way. For the projects in this book done on evenweave linen, I used sizes 24 or 26.

If you're cross-stitching on gingham or waste canvas, however, a sharp-pointed crewel needle (see Decorative Embroidery, page 20) is what you want, since you'll be piercing either the finely woven gingham or the fabric beneath the waste canvas.

Harvest Apron

Nowhere does the practical combine more perfectly with the pretty than in the humble-yet-lovely embroidered apron. Though its mission is, first and foremost, to be a clean-clothes-keeper, the handmade apron belies the essential creativity and appreciation of beauty of the domestic artist hard at work. This sophisticated take on classic cross-stitched gingham uses an Eastern European motif to make a wide border, with the tiny center pattern repeated across the waistband. Fall farm-girl fantasies commence!

Skill Level
EMBROIDERY: Medium
FINISHING: Medium

Finished Size
30" x 26" (76cm x 66cm)
with 29" (74cm) ties

Materials
- CHART
  Harvest Apron chart (page 75)
- FABRIC
  For skirt: One 31" x 31" (79cm x 79cm) piece of ⅛" (3mm) gingham
  For waistband: One 20" x 8" (51cm x 20.5cm) piece of ⅛" (3mm) gingham
  For ties: Two 30" x 4" (76cm x 10cm) pieces of ⅛" (3mm) gingham
- EMBROIDERY THREAD
  DMC cotton 6-strand embroidery floss
- CREWEL NEEDLE
- 4" (10CM) EMBROIDERY HOOP
- AIR-ERASE FABRIC MARKER OR DRESSMAKER'S CHALK
- SEWING THREAD MATCHED TO THE COLOR OF THE FABRIC
- SEWING MACHINE

Thread Guide

COLOR NUMBER		COLOR
351	■	Coral
838	■	Beige Brown, very dark
519	■	Sky Blue

Embroider the skirt

1. Find the center gingham square of the bottom border: Fold the skirt fabric in half lengthwise, then, along this fold, measure 9½" (24cm) from the bottom edge With the marker or chalk, mark this spot as the center square of the center motif.

2. Following the colors indicated in the diagram, embroider this center motif. Position the next motif 5 squares from the edge of the first. You do not need to start embroidering at the center of the subsequent motifs; just start at the bottom corner closest to the motif you've already worked. Continue until you have stitched 2 motifs on either side of the center motif.

Embroider the waistband

1. Find the center gingham square of the waistband border: Fold the waistband in half widthwise, then along this fold, measure 3" (7.5cm) from the bottom edge. With the marker or chalk, mark this spot as the center square of the center motif of the waistband border.

2. Following the colors indicated in the diagram, embroider the center motif. You do not need to start embroidering at the center of the subsequent motifs; just start at the bottom corner closest to the motif you've already worked. Position the next motif 5 squares from the edge of the first. Continue until you have stitched 6 motifs on either side of the center motif. Refer to Finishing (page 154) to clean and press the embroidery on the waistband and the skirt.

Finish the apron

1. On the skirt, hem each long side edge: Turn under each edge ¼" (6mm) and press, repeat the procedure, then machine-stitch close to the edge. Along the bottom edge of the skirt piece, press under ¼" (6mm), and then fold the hem up to the back side of the apron about 6¼" (16cm), centering the embroidered motifs vertically over the hem. By hand, tack the hem to the wrong side of the apron using a hemstitch (see General Sewing Techniques, page 152).

2. Along the top of the skirt piece, mark points 10" (25.5cm) from each side edge. On each side, gather the top of the apron between this point and the side hem until the area is about half its original width.

3. To make the waistband, press under ¼" (6mm) on the short edges. Fold the waistband piece in half lengthwise, with the wrong sides together, and press. Unfold, then fold the long edges in again toward the first fold, and press.

4. To make an apron tie, hem the long edges and the remaining short edge: Turn under each edge ¼" (6mm) and press, then repeat the procedure and stitch. Turn the bottom corner of the short finished edge up to the back of the tie to make a 45-degree angle. Stitch across the top of the turned-under piece to hold the edge in place. Gather the unfinished short edge (you'll stick this edge in the waistband). Repeat for the second tie.

5. With the right side facing you, lay the top edge of the apron skirt inside the folded waistband, making sure the waistband overlaps the apron by about ½" (13mm), and pull up the gathers at each side so that the top edge of the apron is the same width as the waistband. Baste along the bottom edges of the waistband to hold it in place, making sure to catch both the front and the back sides in the stitches. Slide the gathered ends of the ties into the side openings of the waistband, pulling up the gathers to fit. Baste in place. Topstitch around the 3 edges of the waistband. Remove the basting stitches.

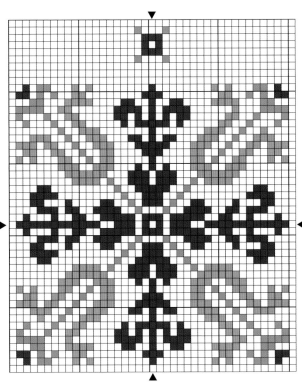

Harvest Apron chart

Use 3 strands of floss throughout.

Thread Guide

COLOR NUMBER	COLOR	
351	▨	Coral
838	■	Beige Brown, very dark
519	▨	Sky Blue

Monogram Album

Waste canvas—a special fabric that allows you to cross stitch on any fabric, regardless of whether or not its weave is even—is a recent discovery in my life. Suddenly, all sorts of projects become possible when you aren't worried about finding appropriate fabric (which I'll admit can be expensive and, unless you're near a great needlework store, comes in a limited palette of colors). Despair no more: Waste canvas makes all sorts of things, including this lovely book cover, easy and inexpensive. ✂ I designed this little monogram and its lacy border to work at a fairly large size, about eight stitches per inch (2.5 centimeters), so that it would feel both rustic and feminine. One initial, simply framed in a five-inch (12.5-centimeter) hoop, makes a perfect, personalized little gift.

Skill Level

EMBROIDERY: Easy
FINISHING: Difficult

Finished Size

Varies, depending on the size of your album

Materials

- CHART
  Simple Monogram chart and Lacy Border chart (opposite)
  One plain hardcover photo album, any size

- FABRIC
  For outside cover: One piece of linen the height of your album plus 1¼" (3cm) x the width of your album (front cover + back cover + spine, measured with the book closed) plus 1½" (3.8cm)

  For lining: One piece of cotton print, cut to the same size as the outside cover piece

  For flaps: Two pieces of linen the height of your album plus 1¼" (3cm) x 5" (12.5cm)

  For trim: Enough ½"- (13mm-) wide rickrack to go around all of the edges of the cover, depending on the size of the album

  For ties: Two 10" (25.5cm) lengths of ½"- (13mm-) wide ribbon

- ONE 6" X 6" (15CM X 15CM) SQUARE OF 8 ½ STITCHES-PER-INCH WASTE CANVAS

- EMBROIDERY THREAD DMC cotton 6-strand embroidery floss

- CREWEL NEEDLE

- MASKING TAPE

- CLEAR PLASTIC RULER

- ROTARY CUTTER

- SELF-HEALING CUTTING MAT

- AIR-ERASE FABRIC MARKER OR DRESSMAKER'S CHALK

- SEWING THREAD MATCHED TO THE COLOR OF THE FABRIC

- SEWING MACHINE

Thread Guide

COLOR NUMBER	COLOR	
823	■	Navy Blue, dark
3865	▨	Winter White

Note: In order to see the Lacy Border chart easily, the colors have been reversed.

Prepare and secure the waste canvas to the fabric

1. To make sure your monogram will be centered on the finished cover, find and mark the center. To do that, first find the center of the album front by measuring the width of the album front and dividing that by 2, then measuring the height of the album front and dividing that by 2. Add ½" (13mm) to each of these two measurements (to account for the seam allowances; don't worry about the extra ease built into the cover fabric measurements—that will just allow the book to fit into the cover more easily). The center point of the front of the cover fabric lies at the intersection of these height and width axes as measured from the bottom right corner of the cover fabric piece. Mark this point with an air-erase fabric marker or dressmaker's chalk, if your fabric is dark.

2. Place masking tape around all four of the edges of the waste canvas. Center the waste canvas over the center point, making sure it is square to the edges of the fabric, and baste it in place around all edges to secure.

Embroider the design

Copy the Lacy Border chart and your preferred letter from the Simple Monogram chart. Carefully cut the monogram out of the paper and tape it, centered, inside the copy of the Lacy Border (when centered horizontally within the border it may be 1 stitch off, but this won't be visible when the monogram is stitched). Following the colors indicated in the diagram, cross-stitch the monogram first, centering it directly over the center point of your front cover, and then stitch the border around the letter. Refer to Finishing (page 154) to clean and press the cover.

Finish the cover

1. For each flap, press in ¼" (6mm) on one long edge, repeat the procedure, and stitch close to the fold. Set the flaps aside.

2. Pin the rickrack trim around the outside edge of the front of the cover fabric, folding the rickrack downward (making a right angle) at each corner and keeping the center of the trim on the seam line,

½" (13mm) from the edge. Baste the rickrack to the cover using a generous ¼" (6mm) seam.

3. For the ties, lay the cover piece facing up on a flat surface. Center the ribbon with the long ends lying loose toward the center of the cover and baste close to the raw edge. With the raw edges even, place the flaps on either end of the cover, right side down. Place the lining, right side down, on top of the stack. Pin ONLY the long edges of the stack and stitch down each long edge using a ½ (13mm) seam.

4. Turn the cover inside out so that the outside piece is on one side and the lining and the flaps are on the other. Press the long edges flat. Flip the flap around so that its right side faces the right side of the outside cover piece. Pin the short edges of the outside piece, flap, and lining, catching the ribbon, and stitch down the edge, using a ½" (13mm) seam. Repeat for the other end of the cover.

5. Trim the corners. Turn the book cover right side out and press.

Lacy Border chart
Use 3 strands of floss throughout.

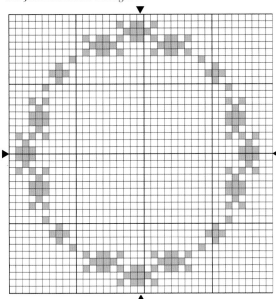

Simple Monogram chart
Use 3 strands of floss throughout.

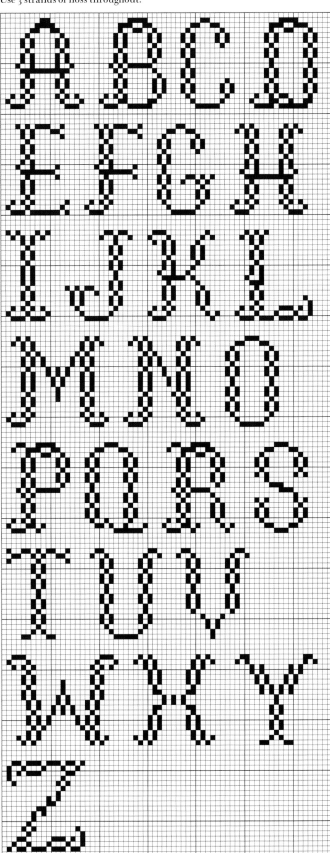

Meadowflower Tote

The feminine details of this pretty bag are so
sweet and fresh. The curling tendrils of the
flower stems echo the gentle curves in this simple
monogram, all done in cross stitch on waste
canvas. Though tiny florals and eyelet
evoke little-girl dresses, this border is laced with
a ¼" (6mm) velvet ribbon for a grown-up touch,
and the neutral-colored linen and dark
charcoal letters further balance the sweetness.
Don't let the delicate details fool you, either—
this tote is generously sized and sturdy enough
for packing a blanket, book, and
blossom-infused beverage. Off to the park
with you, lassie.

Skill Level

EMBROIDERY: Easy

FINISHING: Medium

Finished Size

17" x 13½" (43cm x 34.5cm) with 10¾" (27cm) straps

Materials

- CHART
  Meadowflower Tote chart (page 84)

- FABRIC
  For embroidered panel: One 7" x 14" (18cm x 35.5cm) piece of linen

  For bag front: One 11" x 14" (28cm x 35.5cm) piece of cotton calico

  For bag back and lining: Three 17½" x 14" (44.5cm x 35.5cm) pieces of cotton calico

For trim: One 16" (40.5cm) length of 1"- (2.5cm-) wide eyelet beading lace

For ribbon: One 16" (40.5cm) length of ¼"- (6mm-) wide velvet ribbon, to thread between openings in beading lace. (You may need to adjust the width of this ribbon, depending on the size of the openings in your lace.)

For interlining: One yard 22"- (55 cm-) wide extra-heavy weight stabilizer

For straps: Two 24" (61cm) lengths of ¼" (6mm) leather lacing

- EMBROIDERY THREAD
  DMC cotton 6-strand embroidery floss

- ONE 6" X 12" (15CM X 30.5CM) PIECE OF 8½ STITCHES-PER-INCH WASTE CANVAS
- CREWEL NEEDLE
- MASKING TAPE
- CLEAR PLASTIC RULER
- ROTARY CUTTER
- SELF-HEALING CUTTING MAT
- AIR-ERASE FABRIC MARKER OR DRESSMAKER'S CHALK
- TWEEZERS
- 1/16" (1MM) HAND-HELD HOLE PUNCH
- SEWING THREAD MATCHED TO THE COLOR OF THE FABRIC
- SEWING MACHINE

Thread Guide

COLOR NUMBER		COLOR
581	■	Moss Green
3325	▫	Baby Blue, light
413	■	Pewter Gray, dark
798	■	Delft Blue, dark

Prepare and secure the waste canvas to the fabric

1. To make sure your monogram will be centered on the linen panel, you first need to find and mark the center point on the panel. Fold the fabric in half lengthwise, then in half again widthwise. Mark this point with an air-erase fabric marker or dressmaker's chalk, if your fabric is dark.

2. Place masking tape around all 4 of the edges of the waste canvas. Center the waste canvas over the center point, making sure it is square to the edges of the fabric, and baste it in place to secure.

Prepare the monogram

Make a copy of the chart and cut out the 3 letters you want to use. Find the center of each letter by counting the stitches vertically and horizontally, and mark those stitches on your charts with a pen. Typically, when all 3 letters of the monogram are displayed at

the same size as they are here, the first (or top) letter is the initial of your first name, the second (or middle) is the initial of your middle name, and the third (or bottom) is the initial of your last name.

Embroider the design

1. Stitch the project, following the colors and stitches indicated in the diagram: Begin cross-stitching at the center point of the middle initial, starting at the center mark on the linen panel that you made earlier. To embroider the top initial, count 5 spaces up from the center-top of the middle initial and begin stitching at the center bottom of the top initial, and work your way up. To embroider the third initial, reverse the process, placing the bottom initial 5 spaces below the second, and centering it relative to the other 2.

2. To remove the waste canvas, remove the basting stitches around the edge, and trim the extra waste canvas to within ½" (13mm) of the embroidery. Dampen the waste canvas with a spray bottle of

water, or by holding it briefly under the tap. The waste canvas will soften up when damp. Begin removing each thread individually with tweezers, keeping embroidery flat and pulling threads straight out, not up. Continue removing threads across one side of design, then repeat on the other side, until it is easy to pull the remaining threads out with your fingers. Allow fabric to dry before continuing. Refer to Finishing (page 154) to press the panel.

Make the tote front and back pieces

1. With right sides together, pin left side edge of the linen panel to the right side edge of the bag front calico panel and machine-stitch, using a ¼" (6mm) seam. Press seam toward calico panel.

2. Thread the eyelet trim with ribbon and pin it to the linen, overlapping the seam with the left edge of the eyelet and centering the trim vertically on the panel. Pin, then machine-stitch down each edge of trim, close to edge, with thread matching the color of the eyelet.

3. Cut the stabilizer into two 18" x 20" (45.5cm x 51cm) pieces. Lay the front of the bag on the stabilizer (some stabilizer will stick out from behind the bag front piece; just leave it for now, since it will be easier to sew this way). Pin, then baste around all edges, using a scant ¼" (6mm) seam. Repeat for bag back. Trim away the extra stabilizer from each piece. With the right sides of the bag pieces together, machine-stitch the side edges and the bottom edge of the bag using a ¼" (6mm) seam.

4. Stitch across the corners about 1" (2.5cm) from the edge to create square bottom corners (see General Sewing Techniques, page 148). Turn the bag right side out and push the points toward the center.

Make the lining

With the right sides of the lining pieces together, stitch the short edges using a ¼" (6mm) seam. Stitch across the bottom of the lining, leaving a 6" (15cm) opening through which you will turn the bag. Stitch across the corners about 1" (2.5cm) from the edge to create square bottom corners (see previous step).

Finish the bag

1. With right sides together, place the outer bag into the lining (the outside of the lining will be facing you). With the top edges even, stitch around the top through all layers, using a ¼" (6mm) seam. Pull the outer bag through the opening in the lining. Turn in the edges of the lining opening and machine-sew the opening closed. Turn the lining to the inside and press the top edge of the bag.

2. For the straps, punch 1 hole in the leather lacing ¼" (6mm) from the end of the lacing and another hole 1" (2.5cm) from the end. Repeat on each end of the 2 lengths of lacing. Mark the top edges of the bag 4" (10cm) from each side seam on the front and the back of the bag. Lay the end of 1 strap at 2 of the marks, 1¼" (3cm) from the top of the bag. Using 6 strands of embroidery floss, stitch the strap to the bag through the holes. Repeat for the other 3 strap ends, being careful not to twist the lacing when attaching the opposite ends.

Meadowflower Tote chart
Use 3 strands of floss throughout.

Thread Guide

COLOR NUMBER		COLOR
581	■	Moss Green
3325	▨	Baby Blue, light
413	■	Pewter Gray, dark
798	■	Delft Blue, dark

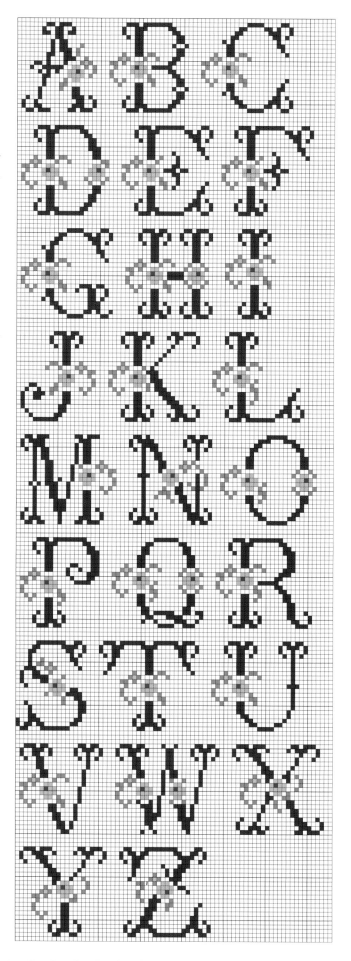

Berry Border Pillow

If you're just learning to do counted cross stitch (or teaching someone, for that matter), gingham's obvious grid offers built-in ease. Available in various sizes of checks, the ⅛" (3mm) size (with eight squares per inch [2.5cm]) is perfect for beginners who aren't yet comfortable stitching on something like unmarked linen, where counting threads takes a bit of practice. This cheerful design, done in primary colors on a dusty-pink gingham background, incorporates a classic "strawberry" border and my own little sunflower-and-hearts motif. I included an inner border of blueberries to really increase the summery, sunshine-y feel of it all.

Skill Level

EMBROIDERY: Easy

FINISHING: Medium

Design Area

Approximately 11" x 11"
(28cm x 28cm)

Finished Size of Cover

To fit a 14" (35.5cm)
square pillow

Materials

- CHART
  Berry Border Pillow chart
  (opposite)

- FABRIC
  For embroidery: One 17" x
  17" (43cm x 43cm)
  piece of ⅛" gingham
  For pillow back: Two
  10" x 14" (25.5cm x
  35.5cm) pieces of printed
  cotton to coordinate with
  embroidered design
  For trim: 1⅔ yd (152.5cm)
  piping trim

- PILLOW FORM
  One 14" x 14" (35.5cm x
  35.5cm) down or down-like
  pillow form

- EMBROIDERY THREAD
  DMC cotton 6-strand
  embroidery floss

- CREWEL NEEDLE

- DRESSMAKER'S CHALK

- 4" (10CM) EMBROIDERY HOOP

- ROTARY CUTTER

- SELF-HEALING CUTTING MAT

- CLEAR PLASTIC RULER

- SEWING THREAD MATCHED
  TO THE COLOR OF THE
  FABRIC

- SEWING MACHINE

Thread Guide

COLOR NUMBER	COLOR	
744		Yellow, pale
580		Moss Green, dark
3840		Lavender Blue, light
154		Grape
321		Christmas Red

Embroider the design

Find the center of the fabric by folding it in half lengthwise, then in half widthwise, and marking the intersection with dressmaker's chalk. Begin in the center of fabric and stitch each motif in cross stitch, working from the center toward the outside of the design area. Stitch the flower first, then the stem and hearts. Stitch the blueberry border next, and finish with the strawberry border.

Finish the pillow

1. Refer to Finishing (page 154) to clean and press the pillow front. Using your ruler, mark a 14" (35.5cm) square on the gingham, centering the design in the square. Please note that gingham fabric, although made of squares, is rarely "square," so just leave about 1½" (3.8cm) of gingham border around the design, and measure again at all 4 corners to make sure the fabric you wind up cutting is perfectly 14" (35.5cm) square. This is the pillow top.

2. With the right sides facing each other, pin the piping trim around the outside edge of the pillow top, with raw edges even and clipping the piping's seam allowance to—but not through—the piping at the corners to turn them sharply. Machine-baste the trim to the top using a scant ¼" (6mm) seam.

3. For the pillow back piece, turn under 1" (2.5cm) on the long edge and press; turn under 1" (2.5cm) again and press. Topstitch along each edge of folded hem. Repeat for the other back piece.

4. With the right side up, lay the pillow front (with the basted trim in place) flat on the work surface. Lay the 2 back pieces right side down on top of the pillow front, overlapping hemmed edges. Pin all thicknesses together around the edges.

5. Machine sew using a ¼" (6mm) seam around the pillow cover, pivoting at the corners. Be careful not to catch the piping in the stitching (just the seam allowance). Clip the corners, turn the pillow cover right side out and press. Stuff with the pillow form and toss it on the bed!

Berry Border Pillow chart
Use 3 strands of floss throughout.

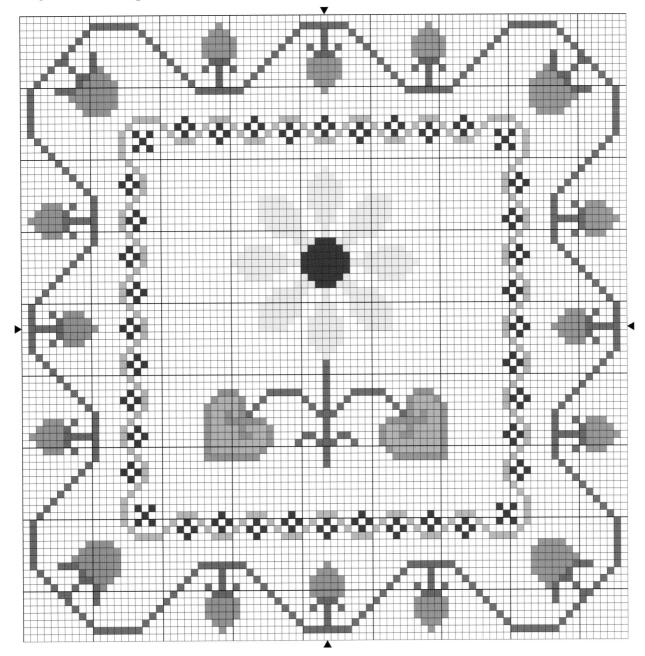

Eyelet Sampler

This small but elegant sampler is a perfect introduction to counted cross stitch on relatively high-thread-count linen. At fourteen stitches per inch, the crosses are still big enough to see clearly, but the use of white floss throughout eliminates the need to fuss with changing colors. Depending on the type of frame you choose, this little collection of delicate motifs would be right at home in almost any setting, which also makes it a perfect gift.

Skill Level

EMBROIDERY: Medium

FINISHING: Easy

Finished Size of Design Area

7¾" x 6½" (20cm x 16.5cm)

Materials

- CHART
  Eyelet Sampler chart (below)
- FABRIC
  One 14" x 13" (35.5cm x 33cm) piece of evenweave linen, 28 count (I used hand-dyed Lakeside Linen in Green Slate)

- EMBROIDERY THREAD
  DMC cotton 6-strand embroidery floss
- TAPESTRY NEEDLE
- 4" (10CM) EMBROIDERY HOOP
- DRESSMAKER'S CHALK

Thread Guide

COLOR NUMBER	COLOR
Blanc	▨ White

Note: In order to see the chart easily, the colors have been reversed.

Embroider the design

Find the center of the fabric by folding it in half lengthwise, then in half widthwise. Begin in the center of fabric and stitch each motif in cross stitch, working from the center toward the outside of the design area. Stitch the eyelet border last.

Finish

Refer to Finishing (page 154) to clean and press the project and finish with a simple wooden frame.

Eyelet Sampler chart
Use 2 strands of floss throughout.

Blossom Napkin

I love the juxtaposition of the rustic quality of oatmeal-colored linen with an organic-though-stylized flower, all bordered by a bit of delicate fringe—that feels like modern homemaking to me. This springtime blossom is done in the corner of a generously cut square of non-evenweave linen—any weight (or color, for that matter) will do, as the waste canvas works its magic here, and allows you to cross-stitch at will. You'll fringe each edge, and finish the border with a simple running stitch, after embroidering. These are quick to do; you'll have your coffee and cookie in no time.

✧ ✧

Skill Level
EMBROIDERY: Easy
FINISHING: Easy

Finished Size of Each Napkin
18" x 18" (45.5cm x 45.5cm)

Materials
- TEMPLATE
  Blossom Napkin chart
  (page 92)

- FABRIC
  For four napkins: One yard (91cm) of 44"- (112cm-) wide (or wider) linen
- EMBROIDERY THREAD
  DMC cotton 6-strand embroidery floss
- ONE 5" X 5" (12.5CM X 12.5CM) SQUARE OF 8½ STITCHES-PER-INCH (2.5 CM) WASTE CANVAS

- MASKING TAPE
- CLEAR PLASTIC RULER
- ROTARY CUTTER
- SELF-HEALING CUTTING MAT
- AIR-ERASE FABRIC MARKER OR DRESSMAKER'S CHALK
- TWEEZERS
- SEWING THREAD MATCHED TO THE COLOR OF THE FABRIC
- SEWING MACHINE
- CREWEL NEEDLE

Thread Guide

COLOR NUMBER		COLOR
224	▢	Shell Pink, very light
3733	▨	Dusty Rose
368	▢	Pistachio Green, light
502	■	Blue Green

✧ ✧

Prepare the fabric

1. Wash and dry the fabric on a normal cycle, removing fabric from dryer while it is still damp. Press it smooth. Using a rotary cutter and self-healing cutting mat, cut the fabric into four 18" x 18" (45.5cm x 45.5cm) squares. Try to cut the edges of each square on the grain of the fabric as much as possible; when you fringe the hem later (by pulling individual threads from the weave of the fabric), you'll thank yourself for fussing here.

2. Using thread the same color as your cloth, machine-sew around all of the edges of the napkin a generous ¼" (6mm) from the raw edge, pivoting at the corners.

These rows of stitches will guide your decorative running stitches, and prevent the frayed edges from fraying too high up the cloth.

Prepare and secure the waste canvas to the fabric

1. To make sure your blossom will be centered on the front of your folded napkin, you first need to find and mark the center point: Fold the napkin in half length-wise, then in half again twice, widthwise. Measure the width of your folded napkin and divide by 2 to find the center axis; on it, measure about 2 ¼" (5.5cm) up from bottom edge. Mark this point with an air-erase fabric marker or dressmaker's chalk, if your fabric is dark.

2. Place masking tape around all 4 of the edges of the waste canvas. Center the waste canvas over the center point of the napkin, making sure it is square to the edges of the fabric, and baste it in place to secure (it will go beyond the edges of the napkin a bit, so just baste directly on the waste canvas on the upper and side edge).

Embroider the design

1. Following the colors indicated in the diagram, cross-stitch the blossom's center first, centering it directly over the center point you marker earlier, then stitch the petals and leaves.

2. To remove the waste canvas, remove the basting stitches around the edge and trim the extra waste canvas to within ½" (13mm) of the embroidery. Dampen the waste canvas with a spray bottle of

water, or by holding it briefly under the tap. The waste canvas will soften up when damp. Begin removing each thread individually with tweezers, keeping embroidery flat and pulling threads straight out, not up. Continue removing threads across one side of design, then repeat on the other side, until it is easy to pull the remaining threads out with your fingers. Allow fabric to dry before continuing.

Finish the napkin

Using 3 strands of color 3733 (Dusty Rose), make running stitches around the entire edge of the napkin, following the inner, machine-sewn line of stitching you created in the first step. To fringe the edges, pull individual threads from each edge up to this line of stitching. Repeat for each napkin. Refer to Finishing (page 154) to clean and press the project.

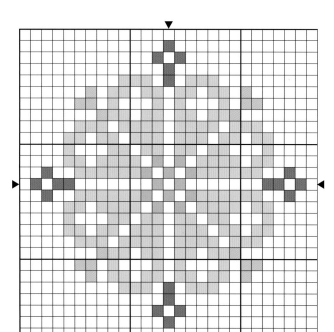

Blossom Napkin chart

Use 3 strands of floss throughout.

Thread Guide

COLOR NUMBER		COLOR
224	▦	Shell Pink, very light
3733	▪	Dusty Rose
368	▦	Pistachio Green, light
502	▪	Blue Green

Olivine Headband

This earthy, folky border in olive green, tomato-soup red, and aqua reminds me of my childhood summers in the 1970s. Stitched on banding—cross-stitch fabric with its edges finished, sold by the yard—this project doesn't require a hoop and the pattern is easily memorized, so it's the perfect take-along. Finished with a simple muslin strip on the wrong side, and a piece of decorative elastic to secure it below, this is a nice, meditative project that, once the embroidery is complete, will come together quickly, ready to wear in no time.

Skill Level
EMBROIDERY: Medium
FINISHING: Medium

Finished Size
15½" x 1½" (39.5cm x 3.8cm) not including elastic

Materials
• TEMPLATE
Olivine Headband chart (page 95)

• FABRIC
For headband: One 18" x 1" (45.5cm x 2.5cm) piece of 14-count cream-colored banding (Measurements do not include finished edges; the stitching area is one inch [2.5 cm].)

For headband backing: One 16¼" x 2¾" (41cm x 7cm) piece of muslin

• EMBROIDERY THREAD
DMC cotton 6-strand embroidery floss

• ONE 8" (20.5CM) LENGTH OF ½" (13MM) DECORATIVE ELASTIC

• TAPESTRY NEEDLE
• SHARP HAND-SEWING NEEDLE
• 3" (7.5 CM) EMBROIDERY HOOP
• AIR-ERASE FABRIC MARKER OR DRESSMAKER'S CHALK
• CLEAR PLASTIC RULER
• ROTARY CUTTER
• SELF-HEALING CUTTING MAT
• LARGE SAFETY PIN
• SEWING THREAD MATCHED TO THE COLOR OF THE BANDING
• SEWING MACHINE

Thread Guide

COLOR NUMBER		COLOR
830	■	Golden Olive, dark
350	■	Coral, medium
470	■	Avocado Green, light
3856	▦	Mahogany, ultra very light
3817	▦	Celadon Green, light
Ecru	□	Ecru

Embroider the design

Find the center of the banding by folding the strip of banding in half widthwise and marking this spot with the marker or chalk. Following the colors indicated on the diagram, begin stitching at the center motif, and work your way to both edges of the design from the center. Refer to Finishing (page 154) to clean and press the banding.

Finish the headband

1. Fold the headband backing in half lengthwise, with the right sides together and the raw edges even. Machine-sew down the length of the headband backing ¼" (6mm) from the raw edges. Attach the safety pin to one end of the backing at the folded edge; snake the safety pin inside the tube of fabric and pull it out the other end to turn the tube right side out. Centering the seam on the back side of the tube, press the long sides of the headband backing smooth.

2. Turn each short end of the tube in ½" (13mm) and press. Turn under the short, raw edges of the headband. With the seam side of the backing facing the wrong side of the headband, on the right side of the headband pin the tube flat to the backing,

centering the headband vertically and horizontally over the tube. Machine-sew, with the right side of headband facing up, down both long edges, keeping the stitches on the finished edge of the band (and not on the embroidery!) and being sure to catch the backing tube in the seam. Take your time here. Leave the short ends open.

3. Insert 1 end of the piece of elastic into 1 end of the tube and baste to secure it temporarily. Place the headband on your head to determine how long the elastic that joins the ends of the headband should be; it should fit comfortably. (This step is easier if you have a helper to hold the headband on for you and mark the elastic's length.) Remove the headband, trim the elastic ½" (13mm) beyond the marked length, insert the elastic into the other end of the tube, and baste to hold.

4. With a sharp needle, hand-sew the ends of the headband closed using a whipstitch (see General Sewing Techniques, page 152), making sure to add a few extra stitches to secure the elastic in the ends of the tube, and the folded edge of the banding to the elastic.

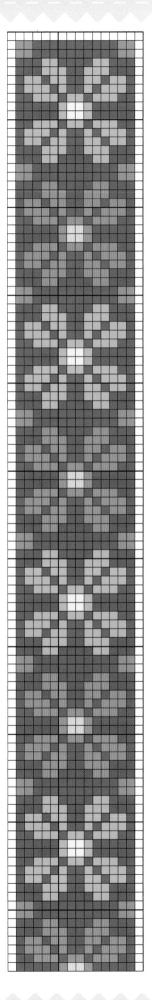

Olivine Headband chart

Use 2 strands of floss throughout.

Thread Guide

COLOR NUMBER		COLOR
830	■	Golden Olive, dark
350	▥	Coral, medium
470	▨	Avocado Green, light
3856	▥	Mahogany, ultra very light
3817	▨	Celadon Green, light
Ecru	□	Ecru

Note: Use mirror image for second half of headband.

Bluegrass Guitar Strap Cozy

My husband has a bluegrass band with his sister, Jen, called the Cavie Creek Scramblers. Never mind that they've only written *one* song (that I know of)—it's a *great* song. I liked it so much that I made him a cross-stitched guitar strap cozy with images from the song (called "County Fair") and the band's monogram. (It was hard to take its picture here because he actually refused to stop singing and playing the guitar.) The designs are stitched on linen banding with finished edges backed with a simple cotton panel that creates a tube— a purchased guitar strap threads right through. May it inspire more tunes.

Skill Level

EMBROIDERY: Medium
FINISHING: Medium

Finished Size

22½" x 2¼" (57cm x 5.5cm) not including guitar strap. This cozy should fit between the parts of the strap that attach to the guitar. If you need to make the embroidered part of the guitar strap shorter, just choose an element or letter to eliminate, or consider spacing the motifs more closely together (depending on how much shorter your strap needs to be).

Materials

• CHART
  Bluegrass Guitar Strap chart (pages 98–100)

• FABRIC
  For cozy: One 26" (66cm) length of 2¼" (5.5cm) linen banding (I used "Celeste" in Sage from Acorns and Threads [see Resources, page 155)

  For strap backing: One 23" x 2¾" (58.5cm x 7cm) piece of cotton

• EMBROIDERY THREAD
  DMC cotton 6-strand embroidery floss

Sampler Threads cotton 6-strand embroidery floss from The Gentle Art

• TAPESTRY NEEDLE

• 3" (7.5CM) EMBROIDERY HOOP

• SEWING THREAD MATCHED TO THE COLOR OF THE FABRIC

• SEWING MACHINE

DMC Thread Guide

COLOR NUMBER		COLOR
3866		Pale Peach
728		Golden Yellow
648		Beaver Gray, light
645		Beaver Gray
564		Jade, very light

The Gentle Art Thread Guide

COLOR NUMBER		COLOR
7008		Rhubarb
1110		Sable
0770		Clover
7034		Gingersnap
1170		Dark Chocolate
0130		Avocado
0390		Buckeye Scarlet

Embroider the design

Beginning in the center of banding, using 2 plies of embroidery floss, cross-stitch each motif, working from the center toward each end of the banding, placing 6 empty spaces between the motifs.

Finish the guitar strap

1. Refer to Finishing (page 154) to clean and press the embroidery. Trim the short ends of the banding so that the motifs are centered vertically, and the final length of the banding is 23 ½" (59.5cm). Fold each short end of the banding in ½" (13mm) and press.

2. Fold each short end of the cotton backing piece in ¼" (6mm) and press. Fold each long end of the cotton backing piece in ¼" (6mm) and press. Lay the banding, wrong side up, on a flat surface. With wrong sides together, pin the folded long edges of the backing to the banding and machine-stitch down each long edge, very close to fold.

3. Thread the guitar strap through the tube created by the banding and the backing so that none of the holes on the strap are covered, and you are able to still attach the strap to the guitar.

Bluegrass Guitar Strap Cozy chart

Use 2 strands of floss throughout.

DMC Thread Guide

COLOR NUMBER		COLOR
3866	▦	Pale Peach
728	▦	Golden Yellow
648	▦	Beaver Gray, light
645	▦	Beaver Gray
564	▦	Jade, very light

The Gentle Art Thread Guide

COLOR NUMBER		COLOR
7008	▦	Rhubarb
1110	▦	Sable
0770	▦	Clover
7034	▦	Gingersnap
1170	▦	Dark Chocolate
0130	▦	Avocado
0390	▦	Buckeye Scarlet

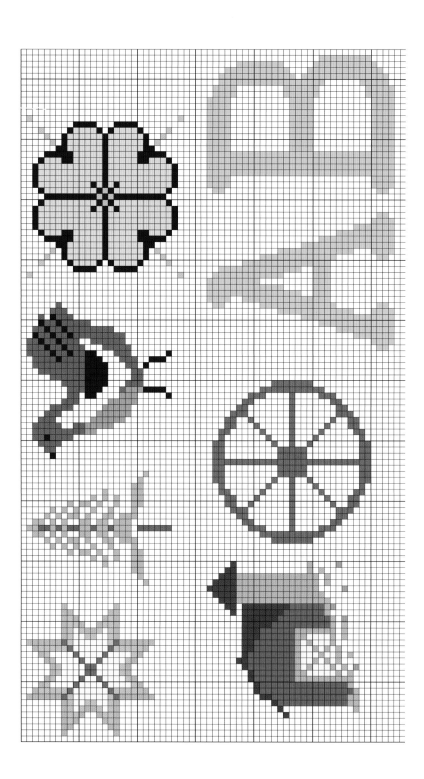

(Refrain:) Let's go to the county fair,
Oh, we're almost there.
Sittin' on a folding chair,
Cowboy hat on if you dare.

Even though we're from the city
The locals don't treat us bad.
The cows and horses look so pretty
Even the drive makes me giddy!

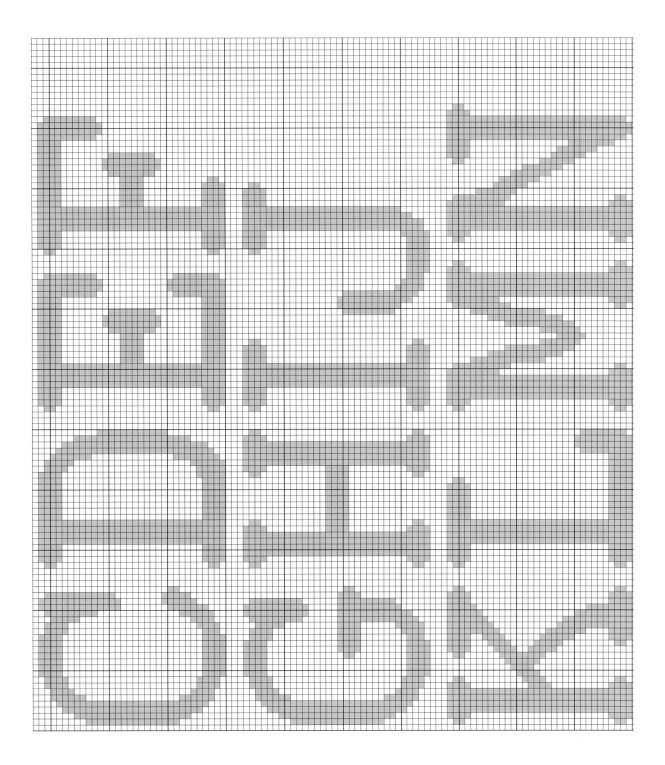

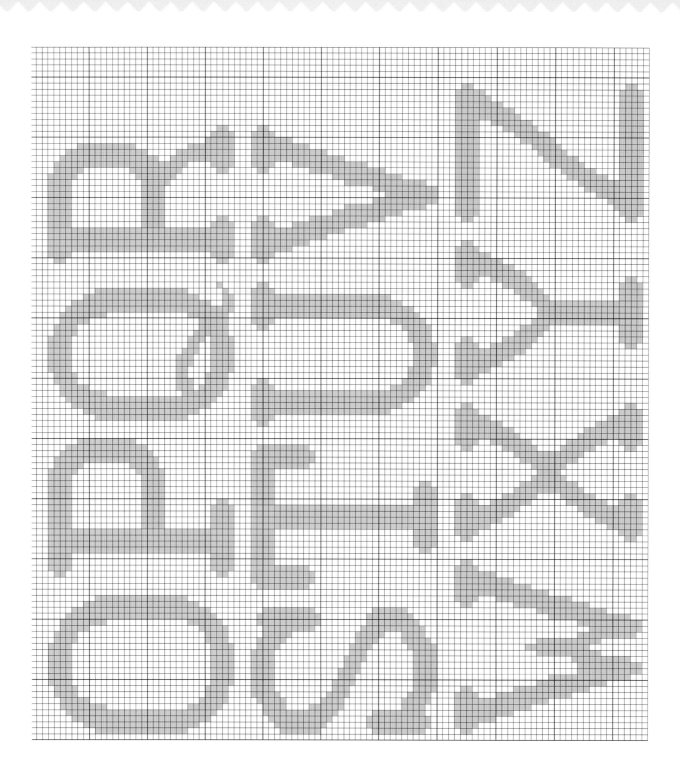

Blackwork Sampler

In a past life, I really think I may have been an Elizabethan seamstress. Of all the exquisite types of embroidery there are to explore, traditional blackwork—a counted-thread embroidery made popular in the sixteenth century by Henry VIII's wife Catherine of Aragon, an accomplished needlewoman—intrigues me to no end. Often done in black silk on a white linen ground, blackwork's geometric motifs are graceful and balanced, filling spaces with delicate, detailed patterns. I am fascinated by how these modest stitches—backstitch and its cousin, the double running stitch, used when both sides of the fabric would show—done in the simplest of colors can create some of the most interesting and intricate (not to mention modern-looking) embroidery I've ever seen. ✄ My little blackwork sampler incorporates nine patterns with varying degrees of detail into a nine-patch square, bordered by cross stitches, done on a ballet-pink ground. Though it seems, at first glance, quite complicated, if you really look at the chart you'll see that each square is made of up smaller repeating motifs, so once you've completed a few simple shapes you can lay the chart aside, and just use your own work to guide you.

Skill Level

EMBROIDERY: Difficult
FINISHING: Easy

Finished Size of Design Area

9" x 9" (23cm x 23cm)

Materials

- CHART
  Blackwork Sampler chart (page 103)
- FABRIC
  One 15" x 13" (38cm x 33cm) piece of evenweave linen, 28 count (I used hand-dyed Zweigart Cashel Linen in Cameo Rose)
- EMBROIDERY THREAD
  DMC cotton 6-strand embroidery floss
- DRESSMAKER'S CHALK
- TAPESTRY NEEDLE
- 4" (10CM) EMBROIDERY HOOP

Thread Guide

COLOR NUMBER	COLOR
310	■ Black

Embroider the design

Find the center of the fabric by folding it in half lengthwise, then in half widthwise, and marking the intersection with dressmaker's chalk. Beginning in the center of fabric, start stitching each square in backstitch, then border it with a row of cross stitches. Work from the center toward the outside of the design area, building squares in relation to each other.

Finish the sampler

Refer to Finishing (page 154) to clean and press the project and finish with a simple wooden frame.

Blackwork Sampler chart

Use 2 strands of floss throughout.

Thread Guide

COLOR NUMBER	COLOR
310	■ Black

Farmstand Baby Bibs

Farm-fresh babies are *soooooooo* cute! These sweet, vintage-y bibs are simple to embroider for them. The strawberry, blueberry, and pear designs on these take advantage of gingham's natural grid to create a polka-dotted effect—the fruit is outlined and filled in with cross stitches, but all of the white squares are left empty. Backed with single-sided pre-quilted cotton, the bib is easy to finish with machine-stitched binding. (Since it will likely be washed frequently, binding it by machine instead of by hand will ensure that the bib can withstand the wear and tear.) Make an un-embroidered bib first, as practice, just to get familiar with stitching binding neatly onto the front before you cut and stitch your embroidered pieces.

Skill Level

EMBROIDERY: Easy
FINISHING: Medium

Finished Size

7½" x 7" (19cm x 18cm) with 12" (30.5cm) ties

Materials

- TEMPLATE AND CHART
  Farmstand Baby Bibs template and chart (page 107)

- FABRIC
  For the embroidery: One 9" x 10" (23cm x 25.5cm) piece of ⅛" (3mm) cotton gingham for each bib

  For backing: One 9" x 10" (23cm x 25.5cm) piece of single-sided quilted cotton for each bib

- For binding and ties: 1½ yd (137cm) of ¼"- (6mm-) wide (when double-folded) double-fold bias tape

- EMBROIDERY THREAD
  DMC cotton 6-strand embroidery floss

- CREWEL NEEDLE

- 4" (10CM) EMBROIDERY HOOP

- FABRIC MARKER

- SEWING THREAD MATCHED TO THE COLOR OF THE BINDING

- SEWING MACHINE

- STRAIGHT PINS

Thread Guide

COLOR NUMBER		COLOR
3064		Desert Sand
744		Yellow, pale
3819		Moss Green, light
164		Forest Green, light
911		Emerald Green, medium
157		Cornflower Blue, very light
158		Cornflower Blue, medium very dark
815		Garnet
817		Coral Red

Prepare the fabric and embroider the design

1. Wash and dry the ginghams on a normal cycle and press them smooth.

2. Copy the Farmstand Baby Bibs template (page 107) at 213% and tape it to a bright window or light box. Trace the outline of the bib onto the gingham fabric with the fabric marker. Do not cut the bib out.

3. Following the colors indicated in the chart, cross-stitch the outline of the fruit on the gingham fabric, centering the fruit on the fabric and being sure to begin the outline on either the colored squares or the white squares as indicated on the photo.

4. Outline the stems, then fill in the leaves or the center of the blueberry stem.

5. Fill in the fruit, leaving all of the white squares empty.

Finish the bib

1. With the wrong sides together, lay the gingham fabric on top of the single-sided quilted fabric. Pin inside the outline of the bib, but do not cut the bib out. Machine-sew through both layers around the outer edge of the bib on the outline. Cut out the bib just outside of the seam, trimming close to (but not through!) the stitches.

2. Cut the binding into two lengths, one 24" (61cm) and one 30" (76cm). Using the shorter length, apply the binding around the bottom edge of the bib, leaving the neck edge unbound. With the right side of the binding facing the right side of the quilted fabric (in other words, the wrong side of the bib), match the raw edge of the unfolded binding to the raw edge of the fabric, and pin along the fold line. Stitch along the fold line, and trim the resulting seam slightly.

Fold the binding over the edge of the bib to the right side, enclosing the raw edges, and pin the folded edge of the binding smoothly. Carefully machine-stitch the binding to the bib through all of the layers, keeping the seam close to folded edge of tape.

3. Find the center of the remaining length of the binding. Matching the center of the binding with the center of the neck edge of the bib, apply the binding as above, along the neck edge with the ends of the binding hanging off of either end of the neck edge (these will be the ties). Open out the binding and fold the short ends in ½" (13mm); refold the binding and pin the ends to hold the hems in place. With bib right side up, beginning at left end of the long tie, machine-stitch down the length of the tie, neatly across the neck edge, and down the other length of the tie, backstitching at each end to secure.

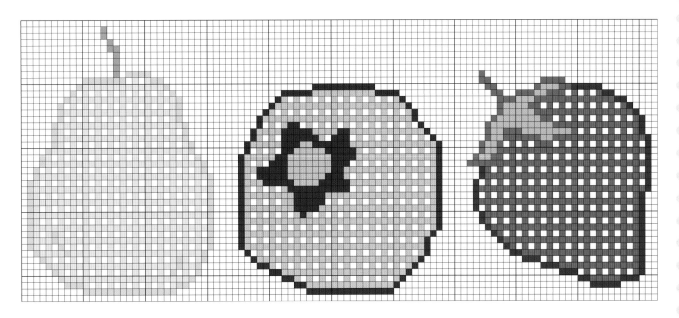

Farmstand Baby Bibs chart

Use 3 strands of floss throughout.

Thread Guide

COLOR NUMBER		COLOR
3064		Desert Sand
744		Yellow, pale
3819		Moss Green, light
164		Forest Green, light
911		Emerald Green, medium
157		Cornflower Blue, very light
158		Cornflower Blue, medium very dark
815		Garnet
817		Coral Red

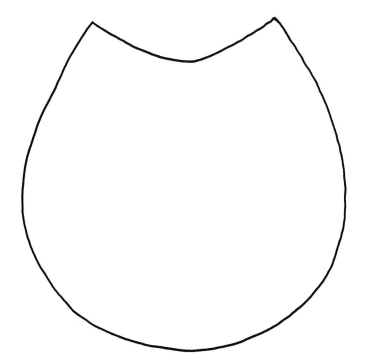

Farmstand Baby Bibs template

Enlarge template by 213%.

Folk Sampler

When I started researching this book, I pored over hundreds of photos of counted cross stitch schoolgirl samplers. The more I looked at them, the more they captivated and intrigued me. The history of these pieces is rich and poignant—many were made by orphans or girls destined to go into service, who learned to stitch alphabets in preparation for monogramming their employers' linens—but each one seems to hold a story we can only guess at now. Letters, numbers, animals, people, cultural motifs, architecture, and natural elements, both stylized and freeform, all figure regularly in samplers, though no two finished pieces are ever alike, each one taking on the personality and charm of (as well as the lessons learned by) its maker. In designing this one, I collected my favorite folk-inspired motifs and colors.

Skill Level

EMBROIDERY:: Difficult

FINISHING: Easy

Finished Size of Design Area

14½" x 13" (37cm x 33cm)

Materials

- CHART

  Folk Sampler chart (pages 110–111)

- FABRIC

  One 21" x 19" (53.5cm x 48.5cm) piece of even-weave linen, 28 count (I used the Cashel linen in Antique White)

- EMBROIDERY THREAD

  DMC cotton 6-strand embroidery floss

- TAPESTRY NEEDLE

- 4" (10CM) EMBROIDERY HOOP

- DRESSMAKER'S CHALK

Thread Guide

COLOR NUMBER		COLOR
3777	■	Terra Cotta, very dark
632	■	Desert Sand, ultra very dark
951	▦	Tawny, light
3863	▦	Mocha Beige, medium
3031	■	Mocha Brown, very dark
729	▦	Old Gold, medium
731	■	Olive Green, dark
3364	▦	Pine Green
646	■	Beaver Gray, dark
927	▦	Gray Green, light
598	▦	Turquoise, light
518	■	Wedgewood, light
3750	■	Antique Blue, very dark
3328	▦	Salmon, dark
760	▦	Salmon

Embroider the design

Find the center of the fabric by folding it in half lengthwise, then in half widthwise, and marking the intersection with dressmaker's chalk. Using 2 strands of floss, begin in the center of fabric and stitch each motif in cross stitch, working from the center toward the outside of the design area. Stitch the outline of the house first, then the door and windows, the roof, and the siding. Then stitch the fence, then the garden.

Stitch the sidewalk, then the flowers, then the people, then animals. To stitch the alphabet, start with the last row, placing the letters in relation to the house, and work up. Stitch the flower border last.

Finish the sampler

Refer to Finishing (page 154) to clean and press the project and finish with a simple wooden frame.

Folk Sampler chart
Use 2 strands of floss
throughout.

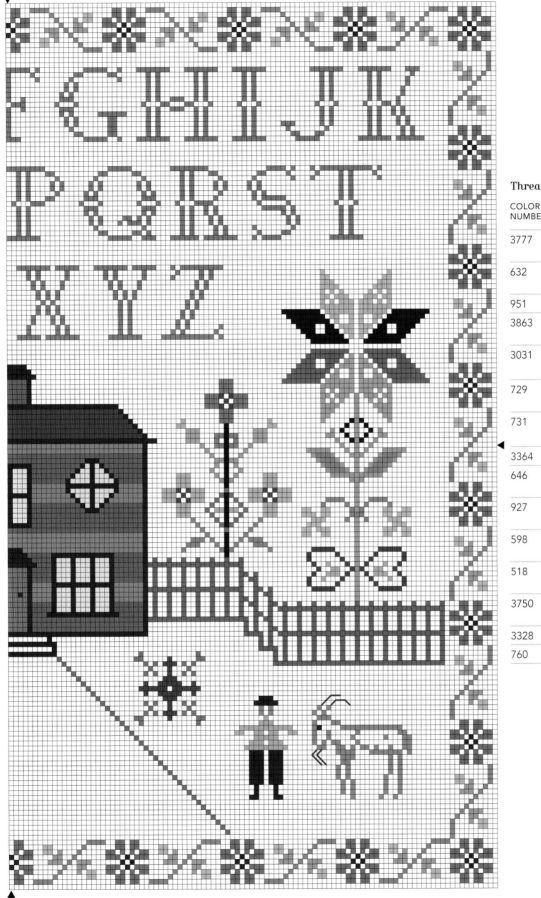

Thread Guide

COLOR NUMBER		COLOR
3777	■	Terra Cotta, very dark
632	■	Desert Sand, ultra very dark
951	▦	Tawny, light
3863	■	Mocha Beige, medium
3031	■	Mocha Brown, very dark
729	▦	Old Gold, medium
731	■	Olive Green, dark
3364	▦	Pine Green
646	■	Beaver Gray, dark
927	▦	Gray Green, light
598	▦	Turquoise, light
518	■	Wedgewood, light
3750	■	Antique Blue, very dark
3328	▦	Salmon, dark
760	▦	Salmon

Karin Curtains

My decorating style has been heavily influenced by nineteenth-century Swedish painter Carl Larsson and his wife, Karin, herself a talented artist and needlewoman. Lilla Hyttnas (Little Furnace), their home in the Swedish countryside, was a lifelong project for the couple—for several decades, they designed and decorated what has become one of the best-loved artist's houses in the world. Filled with flowers, children, pets, and the myriad delicate details that a true artistic vision produces, Lilla Hyttnas was both canvas and muse to the Larssons. In hundreds of watercolors Carl documented the everyday activities of his family and domestic life against this happy backdrop. I like to think these curtains would be right at home there.

Skill Level

EMBROIDERY: Difficult
FINISHING: Medium

Finished Size of Each Curtain

14" (35.5cm) wide; length varies, determined by individual window

Materials

• CHART
  Karin Curtains chart
  (page 115)

• FABRIC
  For each embroidered panel: One 15" x 18" (38cm x 45.5cm) piece of 11-count Aida cloth in Antique White

  For each gathered panel: One piece of ¼" (6mm) gingham, 45" (114cm) wide x the distance from the bottom of your curtain clips to your windowsill

• EMBROIDERY THREAD
  DMC cotton 6-strand embroidery floss
• TAPESTRY NEEDLE
• 4" (10CM) EMBROIDERY HOOP
• STRAIGHT PINS
• DRESSMAKER'S CHALK
• 10 CLIP-ON CURTAIN RINGS
• SEWING THREAD MATCHED TO THE COLOR OF THE FABRIC
• HEAVYWEIGHT THREAD MATCHED TO THE COLOR OF THE FABRIC
• SEWING MACHINE

Thread Guide

COLOR NUMBER	COLOR	
3761	☐	Sky Blue, light
3750	■	Antique Blue, very dark
321	■	Christmas Red

Make the embroidered panel

1. To begin embroidering, find the center of the Aida-cloth panel by folding it in half widthwise. Along this fold, count up 12 squares from the bottom of the panel, and mark this square; this is the center of the dark blue square below the center bottom red flower on the panel. Begin cross-stitching at this point and work out toward the ends.

2. Refer to Finishing (page 154) to clean and press the panel. Fold the panel in half lengthwise, keeping the design on the front. Press under all the raw edges ½" (13mm).

Make the gathered panel

1. To hem the bottom edge, fold under 4" (11.5cm) twice, and pin. By hand, tack the hem to the wrong side of the panel using hemstitch (see General Sewing Techniques, page 152).

2. To gather the top edge, run stitches by hand across the top of the panel, ½" (13mm) from raw edge using heavyweight thread. Gather panel to fit width of embroidered panel.

Finish curtain

1. Insert top of gathered panel between folded bottom edges of embroidered panel. Pin and stitch neatly around all edges of top panel through all layers.

2. Attach clips and hang on rod.

3. Repeat all steps to create the second panel.

Karin Curtains chart

Use 3 strands of floss throughout.

Thread Guide

COLOR NUMBER		COLOR
3761		Sky Blue, light
3750		Antique Blue, very dark
321		Christmas Red

Crewelwork

*C*rewelwork generally refers to decorative embroidery done using woolen yarn to outline and fill in shapes and designs that have been transferred to linen or wool fabric. Crewelwork employs several traditional stitch patterns that lend themselves particularly well to the organic, tactile nature of wool yarn, making it both charmingly old-fashioned, yet modern when revisited in a contemporary setting.

History

Known for its heavily textured stitching, wildly stylized florals, and exotic motifs, crewelwork is one of the most recognizable styles of embroidery. Though the specific origins of crewelwork are hard to trace, the word "crewel" refers to the wool yarn that was used as thread. Wool—widely available, less expensive than fancier silk or imported fibers, and warm—was a popular choice of thread for embellishing clothing and linens.

Through the Middle Ages, embroidery designs and motifs were passed directly from stitcher to stitcher, or through finished items that made their ways from country to country. The first printed embroidery pattern book arrived on the scene in 1523, and for the first time various patterns and designs began circulating in printed form around Europe and the Middle East. Crewelwork became very popular in England, especially during the Elizabethan and Jacobean periods of the mid-sixteenth and early seventeenth centuries, and as the Renaissance shined its light across Europe, a renewed interest in fancy ornamentation in both dress and home decor trickled right down into the hands of amateur enthusiasts. Embroidery became a widely practiced leisure pastime. In the New World, settlers brought wool and hoops across the Atlantic, and an American style of crewelwork inspired by indigenous flora and fauna developed and flourished in the Colonies through the eighteenth century.

Interest in crewelwork then waned, but it enjoyed an enthusiastic revival in the 1960s and 1970s, as both its natural fibers and nostalgia appealed to the Flower Power generation. I admit it—as a child of the 1970s, I love it because it just reminds me so much of home.

Fabrics

Though crewelwork can be done on any type of fabric, closely-woven, heavier fabrics, like linen or woven wools, work (and look) best with crewel yarn. Wool felt, a fabric made of matted and comprised wool and other fibers, can also work well. Generally, crewelwork pieces, even if functional, shouldn't be washed; try spot cleaning for best results here.

Threads

Crewel wool, a soft, two-ply wool yarn, is widely available in hundreds of gorgeous colors and many subtle shades. All of the projects I've designed here use one strand of Appleton crewel wool, though Persian wool, made of three strands, can be substituted. Skeins come in twists of pre-cut lengths. I keep my wools in a big hat box, with the tags to indicate color numbers kept on, and just pull strands out as I need them.

Needles

Sharp, medium-length crewel needles (see Decorative Embroidery, page 20) are the best type to use for crewel-work. I used a size 5 for the projects I've designed here.

Dahlia Field Pillow

There's a gentle quality to this pillow that
I love—it feels like a Midwestern summer night
to me. Inspired by the dahlia fields at our
favorite local farm, I designed this sleepy little
scene to accompany my collection of
mellow-yellow flowered pillowcases from the
1960s. Though the embroidery will take
a bit of doing, the pillow finishes quickly with
a simple envelope back. Find that summer
nightgown and get ready to nap.

Skill Level
EMBROIDERY: Medium
FINISHING: Medium

Finished Size
To fit an 18"- (45.5cm-) square
pillow form

Materials
• TEMPLATE
  Dahlia Field Pillow template
  (page 123)

• FABRIC
  For pillow front: One 18" x 18"
  (45.5cm x 45.5cm) piece of
  blue linen
  For gingham ground: One 18" x
  5" (45.5cm x 12.5cm) piece of
  ½" (13mm) green gingham

For pillow back: Two 14" x 18"
(35.5cm x 45.5cm) pieces of
blue linen

• EMBROIDERY THREAD
  Appleton 2-ply crewel wool
  DMC 6-strand cotton
  embroidery floss

• STRAIGHT PINS

• 2½ YD (229CM) OF PIPING TRIM

• 18" X 18" (45.5CM X 45.5CM)
  PILLOW FORM

• CREWEL NEEDLE

• 4" (10CM) EMBROIDERY HOOP

• SEWING THREAD MATCHED TO
  THE COLOR OF THE FABRIC

• SEWING MACHINE

Appleton Thread Guide

COLOR NUMBER		COLOR
944	■	Carnation Pink, medium dark
244	■	Moss Green, dark
707	□	Soft Cream Pink, medium
882	□	Orchid Lights Yellow
692	▦	Palomino Gold, very light
471	□	Marigold Yellow, very light
941	▨	Carnation Pink, very light
353	▨	Grey Green, medium light
331	■	Drab Green, very light
543	■	Early English Green, light
332	□	Drab Green, light
946	■	Bright Rose Pink, medium dark
876	▢	Pastel Blue, light
997	▦	Gold
502	■	Scarlet, light
701	□	Flesh Tint, ultra very light
695	▨	Honeysuckle, medium

DMC Thread Guide

COLOR NUMBER		COLOR
3371	■	Black Brown
3340	■	Apricot, medium
3609	▨	Plum, ultra light
745	□	Yellow, light pale

Prepare fabric and transfer the design

1. To prepare the front of the pillow, with right sides facing, lay the gingham across the front of the pillow with the bottom edge of the gingham 4 ½" (11.5cm) from the bottom edge of the pillow front. Stitch along bottom edge of gingham piece ½" (13mm) from raw edge. Fold the gingham down over the seam and press flat. To keep the pieces of the fabric together and the edges of your fabric from unraveling while you work, machine zigzag or overlock stitch to bind the raw edges around all sides.

2. Copy the template, enlarging it 154%, and cut the design from the paper, leaving a ¼" (6mm) margin.

3. Select a transfer technique (see Transferring Designs, page 16) and transfer the design to the linen.

Embroider the design

Stitch the project, following the colors and stitches indicated in the diagram. Refer to Finishing (page 154) to clean and press the pillow front.

Finish the pillow

1. Pin the piping trim around the outside edge of the pillow top, raw edges even and clipping piping seam allowance almost to the piping at the corners to turn them sharply. Machine-baste the trim to the top using a scant ¼" (6mm) seam.

2. For the pillow back pieces, on 1 back piece turn under 1" (2.5cm) on the long edge and press; turn under 1" (2.5cm) again and press. Topstitch along each edge of the hem. Repeat for the other back piece.

3. With the right side up, lay the pillow front (with the basted trim in place) flat on the work surface. Lay the 2 back pieces right side down on top of the pillow front, overlapping the hemmed edges. Pin all thicknesses together around the edges.

4. Machine-sew using a ¼" (6mm) seam around the pillowcase, pivoting at the corners. Be careful not to catch the piping in the stitching (just catch the seam allowance). Clip the corners, turn the pillow cover right side out, and press. Stuff with the pillow form.

Dahlia Field Pillow template

Use 1 strand of wool and 2 strands of floss throughout.
See page 14 for stitch abbreviations.
Enlarge template by 154%.

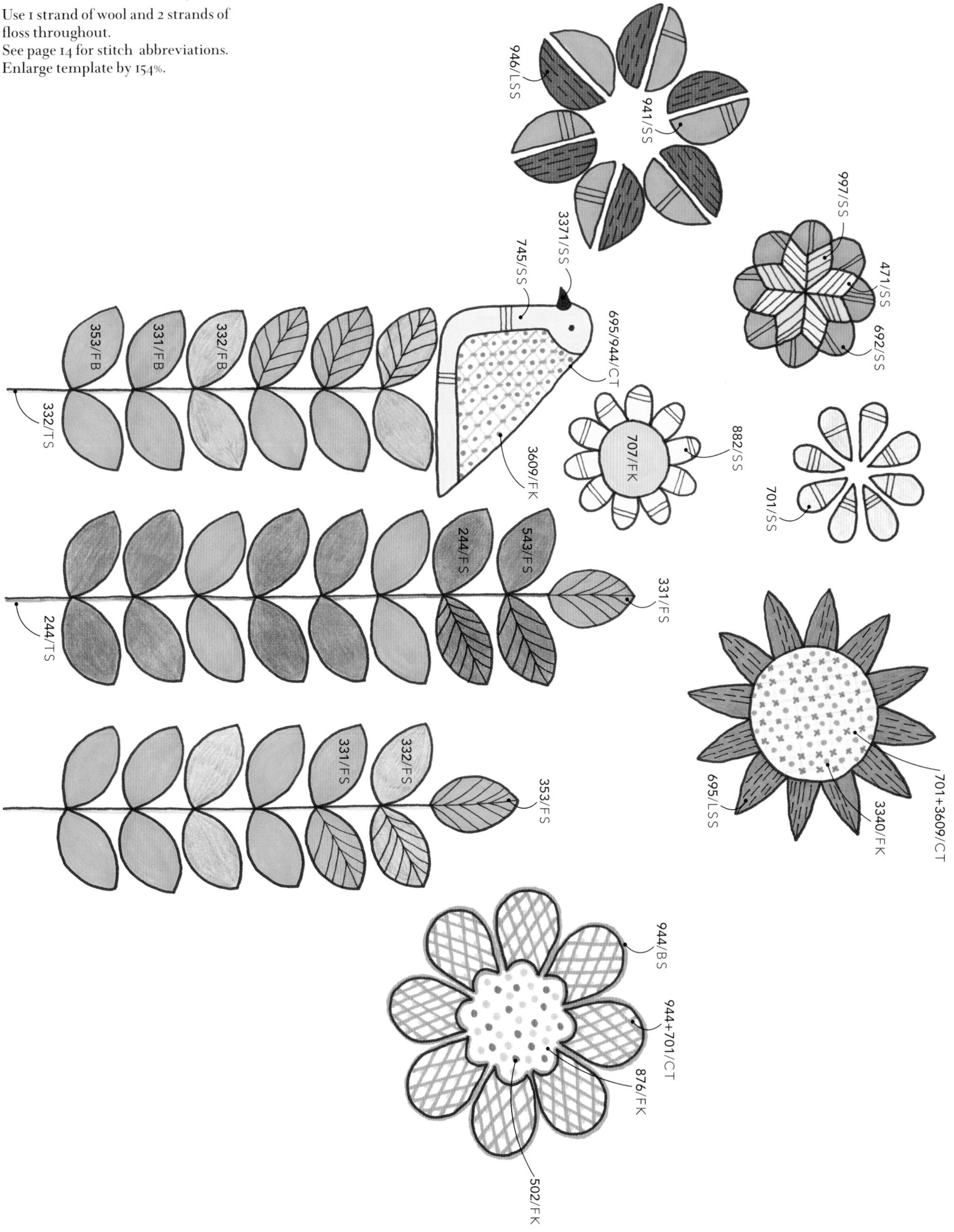

946/LSS

941/SS

3371/SS

745/SS

997/SS

471/SS

692/SS

353/FB

331/FB

332/FB

332/TS

695/944/CT

3609/FK

882/SS

701/SS

707/FK

244/FS

543/FS

331/FS

244/TS

331/FS

332/FS

353/FS

695/LSS

701+3609/CT

3340/FK

944/BS

944+701/CT

876/FK

502/FK

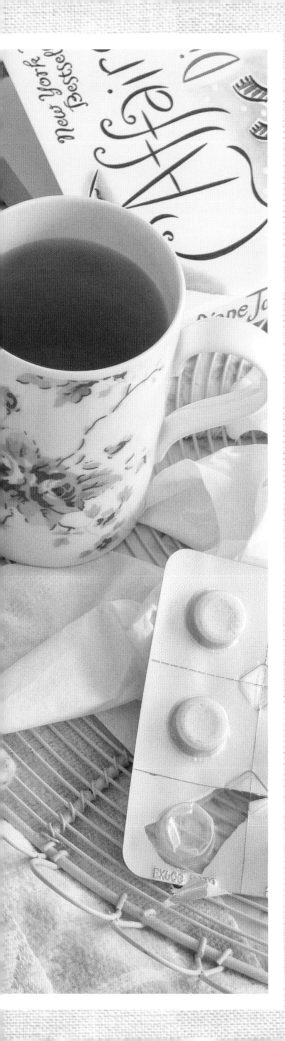

Snowflake and Pine Tree Hot Water Bottle Covers

The basement furnace that warms our little 1927 house has a hard time sending heat upstairs to the second floor, and then across the room to our bed, which is perched under a huge set of original (read: draughty) double-hung (read: very draughty) windows. So in the middle of winter, something we liked to do (yes, we are dorks) is fight over the dog and the one hot water bottle we had in our possession. Then I got smart and purchased one for each of us and made snuggly soft flannel and cashmere covers embroidered with snow for me, trees for him. Clover Meadow Paulson is really not understanding why anyone needs a hot water bottle with her around.
Good question.

Skill Level

EMBROIDERY: Easy
FINISHING: Medium

Finished Size

9" x 14¾" (23cm x 37.5cm)

Materials

- TEMPLATE
  Snowflake or Pine Tree template (page 128)

- FABRIC
  For embroidered panel and center back panel:
  Two 9½" x 6½" (24cm x 16.5cm) pieces of cashmere or very soft woven wool

  For top panels: Two 9½" x 6½" (24cm x 16.5cm) pieces of flannel

  For bottom panels: Two 9½" x 3½" (24cm x 9cm) pieces of flannel

  For lining: Two 9½" x 16" (24cm x 40cm) pieces of flannel

  For ties: 1 yd (91cm) of ½"- (13mm-) wide twill tape or ribbon

  Note: These measurements will make a bag that is intended to fit a standard American hot water bottle measuring 8" (20.5cm) wide by 10" (25.5cm) tall, with a 3" (7.5cm) neck. If your bottle is a different size, adjust the width and the bottom panels accordingly.

- EMBROIDERY THREAD
  Appleton 2-ply crewel wool
- DRESSMAKER'S CHALK
- CREWEL NEEDLE
- 4" (10CM) EMBROIDERY HOOP
- SAFETY PIN OR BODKIN
- SEWING THREAD MATCHED TO THE COLOR OF THE FABRIC
- SEWING MACHINE

Thread Guide

COLOR NUMBER		COLOR
882	☐	Orchid Lights Yellow
991	☐	White
253	◻	Leaf Green, medium
353	◻	Grey Green, medium light
244	◼	Moss Green, dark
314	◻	Yellow Ochre, medium
588	◼	Burnt Umber, very dark

Prepare fabric and transfer the design

1. Copy the template, enlarging it 125% (for Snowflake) or 115% (for Pine Tree), and cut out 1 snowflake or pine tree on the outline.

2. To transfer the design to the wool, first find the center of the panel by folding it in half lengthwise and widthwise, and marking this point with chalk. Center the snowflake or pine tree over this point, and trace carefully around the paper using dressmaker's chalk. Then center the shape to 1 side, and trace, and repeat for the other. You can use a ruler for exact placement, but I prefer to just eyeball it. You can also use a marker to draw lightly over your chalk outline if necessary.

Embroider the design

Stitch the project, following the colors and stitches indicated in the diagram. Refer to Finishing (page 154) to clean and press the project.

Make the bag

1. Press around the stitching so that the fabric is smooth. With right sides together and using a ¼" (6mm) seam, stitch the long side of the top panel to the top edge of the embroidered panel and the long side of the bottom panel to the bottom edge of the embroidered panel. Repeat for back pieces.

2. With the right sides of the bag front and bag back together, mark a 1" (2.5cm) opening on the right seamline, 2 ¼" (7cm) from the top edge of the bag. Using a ¼" (6mm) seam, stitch the 2 side seams, backstitching around both sides of the opening (do not close the seam here).

3. Stitch across the corners about 1" (2.5cm) from the edge to create square bottom corners (see General Sewing Techniques, page 152). Turn the bag right side out and push the points toward the bottom center of the bag.

Make the lining

With the right sides of the lining pieces together, stitch the long edges using a ¼" (6mm) seam. Stitch across the bottom of the lining, leaving a 4" (10cm) opening through which you will turn the bag. Stitch across the corners about 1" (2.5cm) from the edge to create square bottom corners (see previous step).

Finish the bag

1. With right sides together, place the outer bag into the lining (the outside of the lining will be facing you). With the top edges even, stitch around the top through all layers, using a ½" (13mm) seam. Pull the outer bag through the opening in the lining. Turn in the edges of the lining opening and machine-sew the opening closed. Turn the lining to the inside and press the top edge of the bag, folding the lining down into the bag.

2. To make the casing for the ties, find the opening you left on the right side seam. With the outside of the bag facing you, stitch 2 straight rows, 1" (2.5cm) apart, through both layers of the fabric. These rows should be parallel to each other and to the top of the bag.

3. To run the tie through the casing, attach a safety pin or bodkin to 1 end of the ribbon or twill tape. Feed the ribbon through the casing, around the bag and back out the opening, centering the tape within the bag. Pull the ties to close.

Snowflake and Pine Tree templates

Use 1 strand of wool throughout.
See page 14 for stitch abbreviations.
Enlarge template by 125% (Snowflake)
and 115% (Pine Tree).

Thread Guide

COLOR NUMBER		COLOR
882	☐	Orchid Lights Yellow
991	☐	White
253	◼	Leaf Green, medium
353	▨	Grey Green, medium light
244	◼	Moss Green, dark
314	▥	Yellow Ochre, medium
588	◼	Burnt Umber, very dark

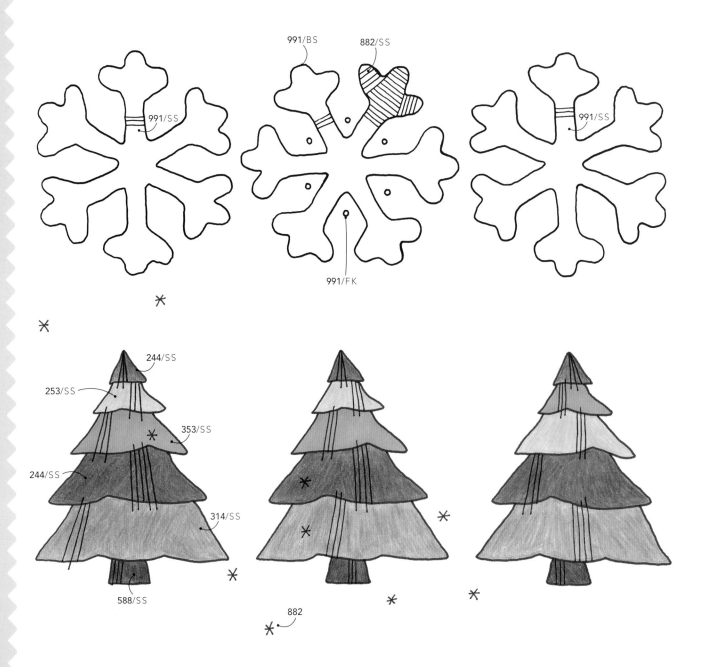

Tree of Life

A generous blogger friend sent me a book of Swedish embroidery designs from the 1950s. I was entranced by the cover image—a traditional motif called a "tree of life," frequently depicted in crewelwork and other needlework and folk designs. Inspired by it, I designed my own version, characterized by the typical stylized branches and leaves, oversized birds and flowers, and a folksy couple in traditional dress. ✂ While not particularly difficult, the large scale of this design will allow you to really settle in with these classic stitches. And crewel goes quickly—that thicker yarn really stacks up quickly compared to embroidery floss (though this design would look beautiful done in cotton floss as well).

Skill Level

EMBROIDERY: Medium

FINISHING: Easy

Finished Size of Design Area

17" x 23" (43cm x 58.5cm)

Materials

- TEMPLATE
Tree of Life template (pages 131–133)

- FABRIC
One 23" x 29" (58.5cm x 74cm) piece of linen

- EMBROIDERY THREAD
Appleton 2-ply crewel wool

- CREWEL NEEDLE
- 4" (10CM) EMBROIDERY HOOP

Thread Guide

COLOR NUMBER		COLOR	COLOR NUMBER		COLOR
944		Carnation Pink, medium dark	543		Leaf Green, medium
244		Moss Green, dark	567		Iris Blue, dark
707		Soft Cream Pink, medium	471		Marigold Yellow, very light
831		Teal Green, light	941		Carnation Pink, very light
882		Orchid Lights Yellow	314		Ochre, medium dark
302		Antique Brown, light	564		Iris Blue, medium
692		Palomino Gold, very light	987		Taupe Gray
			584		Burnt Umber, very dark

Prepare fabric and transfer the design

1. To keep the edges of your fabric from unraveling while you work, machine zigzag or overlock stitch to bind the raw edges around all sides.

2. Copy the template, enlarging it 167%, and assemble according to instructions. Cut the design from the paper, leaving a ¼" (6mm) margin. You may have to tape several sheets of paper together, matching design lines where necessary.

3. Select a transfer technique (see Transferring Designs, page 16) and transfer the design to the linen.

Embroider the design

Stitch the project, following the colors and stitches indicated in the diagram. Outline all shapes using color 584 (Burnt Umber, very dark) and backstitch.

Finish the project

Refer to Finishing (page 154) to clean and press the project and finish with a simple wooden frame.

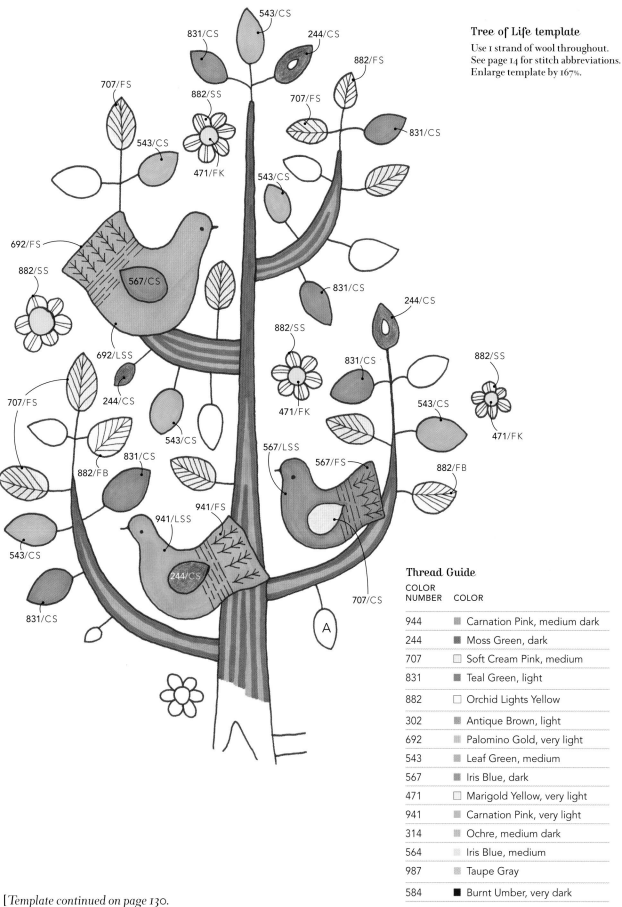

Tree of Life template
Use 1 strand of wool throughout.
See page 14 for stitch abbreviations.
Enlarge template by 167%.

543/CS
831/CS
244/CS
882/FS
707/FS
882/SS
707/FS
831/CS
543/CS
471/FK
543/CS
692/FS
567/CS
882/SS
831/CS
244/CS
882/SS
831/CS
882/SS
692/LSS
707/FS
244/CS
543/CS
471/FK
543/CS
471/FK
882/FB
831/CS
567/LSS
567/FS
882/FB
941/FS
543/CS
941/LSS
244/CS
707/CS
831/CS

A

Thread Guide

COLOR NUMBER		COLOR
944		Carnation Pink, medium dark
244		Moss Green, dark
707		Soft Cream Pink, medium
831		Teal Green, light
882		Orchid Lights Yellow
302		Antique Brown, light
692		Palomino Gold, very light
543		Leaf Green, medium
567		Iris Blue, dark
471		Marigold Yellow, very light
941		Carnation Pink, very light
314		Ochre, medium dark
564		Iris Blue, medium
987		Taupe Gray
584		Burnt Umber, very dark

[*Template continued on page 130.*
To assemble, align A over A and B over B.]

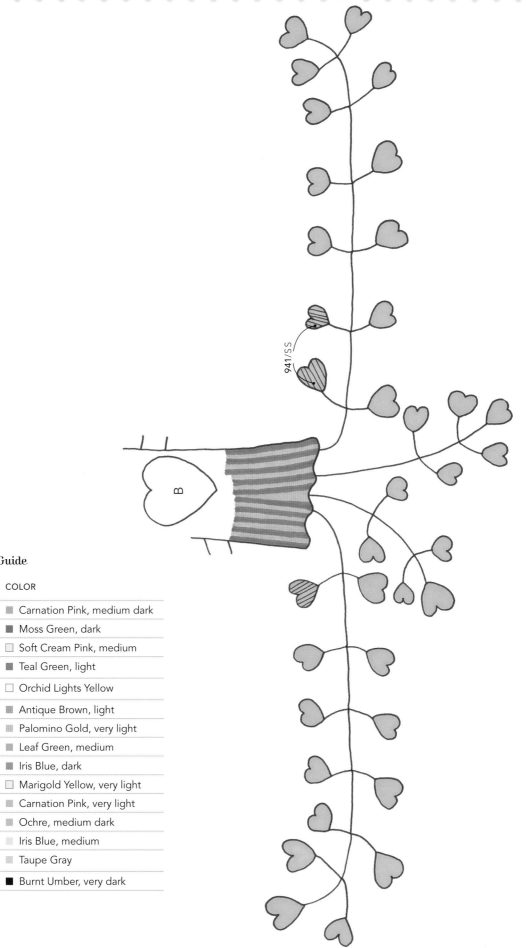

Thread Guide

COLOR NUMBER		COLOR
944		Carnation Pink, medium dark
244		Moss Green, dark
707		Soft Cream Pink, medium
831		Teal Green, light
882		Orchid Lights Yellow
302		Antique Brown, light
692		Palomino Gold, very light
543		Leaf Green, medium
567		Iris Blue, dark
471		Marigold Yellow, very light
941		Carnation Pink, very light
314		Ochre, medium dark
564		Iris Blue, medium
987		Taupe Gray
584		Burnt Umber, very dark

Woodland in Wool

This traditional crewelwork design is taken from an early American seat cushion from the 1730s. Complete with oversized exotic blossoms and strangely peaceful creatures from the animal kingdom (peaceful, given that predator and prey are in such close proximity and all), the classic elements in this scene are good examples of the stylized fantasy present in many of these kinds of heavily detailed crewelwork pieces. I started and finished this piece during a weeklong snowstorm. The juxtaposition of the wool paired with such a tropical scene mirrored my warm-weather dreams.

Skill Level

EMBROIDERY: Difficult
FINISHING: Easy

Finished Size of Design Area

14" x 11" (35.5cm x 28cm)

Materials

- TEMPLATE
  Woodland in Wool
  template (pages 136–137)
- FABRIC
  One 20" x 17" (51cm x 43cm) piece of white linen
- EMBROIDERY THREAD
  Appleton 2-ply crewel wool
- CREWEL NEEDLE
- 4" (10CM) EMBROIDERY HOOP

Thread Guide

COLOR NUMBER		COLOR		COLOR NUMBER		COLOR
944	▫	Carnation Pink, medium dark		332	▫	Drab Green, light
244	■	Moss Green, dark		502	▫	Scarlet, light
707	▫	Soft Cream Pink, medium		695	▫	Honeysuckle, medium
831	■	Teal Green, light		432	▫	Signal Green, very light
302	■	Antique Brown, light		348	■	Mid Olive Green, very dark
471	▫	Marigold Yellow, very light		563	▫	Sky Blue, light
941	▫	Carnation Pink, very light		561	▫	Sky Blue, ultra very light
564	▫	Iris Blue, medium		567	■	Sky Blue, dark
987	▫	Taupe Gray		905	■	Golden Brown, dark
353	▫	Grey Green, medium light		866	■	Coral, medium dark
331	▫	Drab Green, very light		503	▫	Scarlet, medium light
543	▫	Early English Green, light		584	■	Brown Groundings, medium light

Prepare fabric and transfer the design

1. To keep the edges of your fabric from unraveling while you work, machine zigzag or overlock stitch to bind the raw edges around all sides.

2. Copy the template, enlarging it 108%, and cut the design from the paper, leaving a ¼" (6mm) margin. You may have to tape several sheets of paper together, matching design lines where necessary.

3. Select a transfer technique (see Transferring Designs, page 16) and transfer the design to the linen.

Embroider the design

Stitch the project, following the colors and stitches indicated in the diagram.

Finish the project

Refer to Finishing (page 154) to clean and press the embroidery and finish with a simple wooden frame.

Woodland in Wool template

Use 1 strand of wool throughout.
See page 14 for stitch abbreviations.
Enlarge template by 108%.

Thread Guide

COLOR NUMBER		COLOR
944		Carnation Pink, medium dark
244		Moss Green, dark
707		Soft Cream Pink, medium
831		Teal Green, light
302		Antique Brown, light
471		Marigold Yellow, very light
941		Carnation Pink, very light
564		Iris Blue, medium
987		Taupe Gray
353		Grey Green, medium light
331		Drab Green, very light
543		Early English Green, light
332		Drab Green, light
502		Scarlet, light
695		Honeysuckle, medium
432		Signal Green, very light
348		Mid Olive Green, very dark
563		Sky Blue, light
561		Sky Blue, ultra very light
567		Sky Blue, dark
905		Golden Brown, dark
866		Coral, medium dark
503		Scarlet, medium light
584		Brown Groundings, medium light

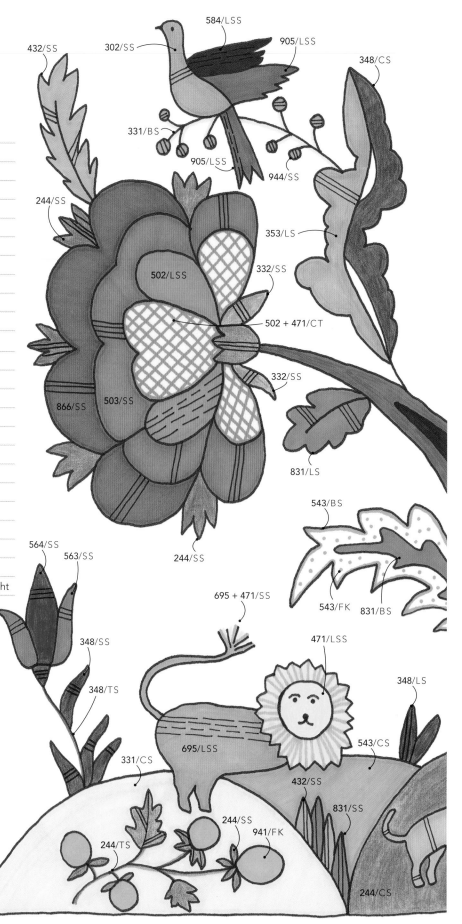

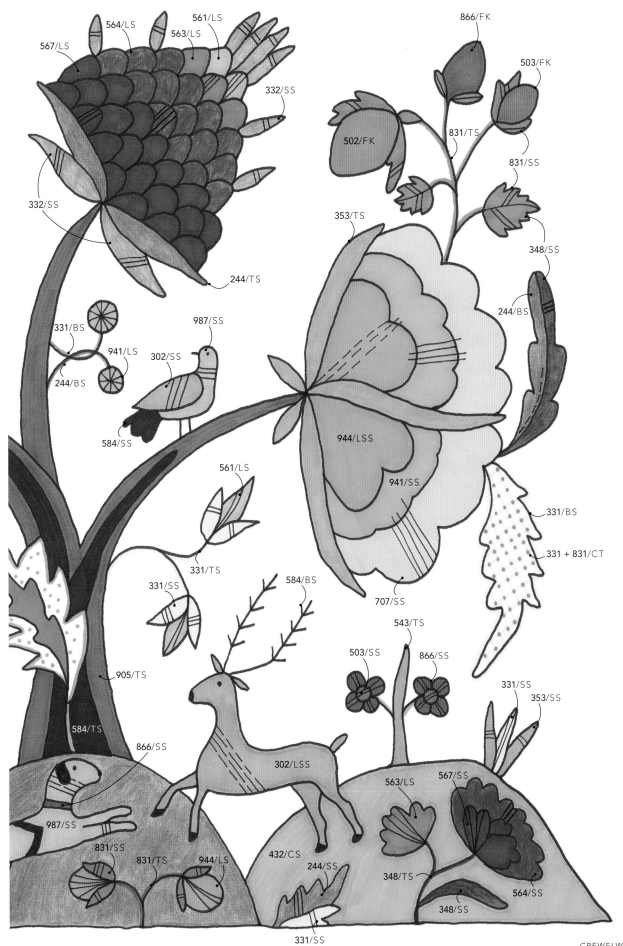

Clover's Quilt

This boucle-inspired monogram is made
entirely of individual French knots that, when
packed tightly together, give these letters
a nubby, retro feel. The throw, patched
together out of various wools, is simple to put
together—there's no batting layer,
and once the top is finished, you simply stitch
it to the calico backing and turn it all right
side out. Then simply pop in a DVD to watch,
and waddle along with your needle,
making a line of running stitches near the
seam to keep the whole thing flat.
Since there's no batting that needs to be held
in place, I didn't bother tying or quilting
each square, but you certainly could.
And consider making this throw into a
bed-sized winter blanket—it's easy to resize,
incorporating any random tweedy pieces
you might have around. ✂ Yes, I made it for
the dog. Don't judge me.

Skill Level

EMBROIDERY: Medium
FINISHING: Medium

Finished Size

55" x 55" (139cm x 139cm)

Materials

- TEMPLATE
  Use your computer for an easy way to create this monogram. Just choose a simple font—I used Courier—and size the letters to about 1½" (3.8cm) tall.

- FABRIC
  For top: Twenty-five 12" x 12" (30.5cm x 30.5cm) pieces of various soft woven wools
  For backing: 3½ yds (3.2m) 45"- (114cm-) wide cotton calico

- EMBROIDERY THREAD
  Appleton 2-ply crewel wool
  DMC six-strand cotton embroidery floss

- ROTARY CUTTER

- SELF-HEALING CUTTING MAT
- CLEAR PLASTIC RULER
- DRESSMAKER'S CHALK PENCIL
- CREWEL NEEDLE
- 4" (10CM) EMBROIDERY HOOP
- STRAIGHT PINS
- 50 MEDIUM-SIZED SAFETY PINS

Appleton Thread Guide

COLOR NUMBER	COLOR
503	■ Scarlet

DMC Thread Guide

COLOR NUMBER	COLOR
DMC 813	▩ Blue, light

Prepare fabric and transfer the design

1. Print out the letters you are going to use, and cut them out on their outlines.

2. To transfer the design to 1 of the squares of wool, first find the diagonal center of the block by folding it in half from corner to corner and pressing lightly with your fingers so that you can just see the crease. Center the middle letter of your monogram on this crease toward the lower corner of the square (remembering that the ½" (13mm) seam allowances will take up some of the margin), and trace carefully around the paper with the dressmaker's chalk. Then center the other letters to either side, and trace each of them. You can use a ruler for exact placement, but I prefer to just eyeball it. You can use a marker to draw lightly over your chalk outline once it is transferred.

Embroider the design

Using 1 strand of wool and French knots, first outline and then fill each initial with tightly-packed stitches.

Make the quilt top

1. With the right sides together and using a ½" (13mm) seam, stitch all the squares into strips of 5, keeping the piece with the monogram facing toward the outside edge of the quilt at the end of one strip. You should have 5 strips of 5 patches each when you are finished. Don't bother trying to press the seams open; it won't work very well, so I'd just skip it.

2. Lay out the 5 strips, right sides up and parallel, on a flat surface until the arrangement pleases you, keeping the monogram in one corner of the throw. Then, starting at 1 end, pin (with straight pins) 2 strips together, right sides facing and seams matching. Stitch down the length. Repeat for each strip, adding a new strip to the ever-growing quilt top, one after another.

3. Cut the length of backing fabric into 2 equal lengths, and seam them together along the long edges to create a piece big enough to back the quilt. Lay the backing fabric right side up on a flat surface. Place the quilt top right side down on top of the back piece. (The quilt top will be smaller than the back piece.) Starting in the center of the quilt, pin a safety pin through the center of each square and then evenly around all of the edges of the quilt, pinning both layers together smoothly.

4. Machine-stitch around all edges through both layers, using a seam that's ½" (13mm) from wool edges and leaving an 8" (20.5cm) opening on one side of the quilt (not at a corner). Trim excess backing, making sure your edges are straight. Turn quilt through opening so that the right side is facing out, then push corners out gently with a crochet hook or other point-turning instrument. Close opening by hand using a blind hemstitch (see General Sewing Techniques, page 152).

5. Thread a sharp needle with a long length of embroidery floss (use all 6 strands) and make running stitches around outside edge of quilt, ½" (13mm) from edge. To start a new length, do not knot the thread, but run the needle for 1" (2.5cm) or so under the layer of fabric, then pull needle and thread out, leaving tail of thread buried inside the quilt; take a small, almost imperceptible stitch on the wrong side of the quilt. To finish a length, reverse the process, taking a small stitch, then running the needle under the fabric and pulling it out 1" (2.5cm) away, and clipping the thread close to the surface.

Gingerbread Heart Mobile

I absolutely adore gingerbread, and gingerbread heart cookies just conjure images of Kristkindl markets in the Black Forest (complete with spiced wine and roasted almonds) at holiday time. *These* confections you can keep for years: They're made of wool felt sandwiched around a cardboard heart, and "iced" with both crewel wool and cotton floss. The backs of the cookies are plain, and three designs repeat twice; when you've finished stitching them up, you'll attach the "cookies" to their grapevine wreath with gingham ribbon. Whip up some heart-shaped waffles for a Christmas-morning breakfast, and hope for snow.

Skill Level

EMBROIDERY: Medium

FINISHING: Medium

Finished Size

Approximately 18" x 22"
(45.5cm x 56cm) per mobile

Materials

- TEMPLATE
  Gingerbread Heart Mobile
  template (opposite)

- FABRIC
  ⅓ yd (30.5cm) 36"- (91cm)
  wide wool or wool-blend
  gingerbread-colored felt, cut
  into twelve 6" x 6" (15cm x
  15cm) squares

- EMBROIDERY THREAD
  Appleton 2-ply crewel wool
  DMC cotton 6-strand
  embroidery floss

- SIX 6" X 6" (15CM X 15CM)
  SQUARES OF THICK
  CARDBOARD (an old
  cardboard box works
  perfectly here)

- 4 YDS (3.6M) ½"- (13MM-) WIDE
  RED GINGHAM RIBBON, CUT
  INTO TWELVE 12" (30.5CM)
  LENGTHS

- ONE 12" (30.5CM)
  GRAPEVINE WREATH

- CREWEL NEEDLE

- FABRIC GLUE

Appleton Thread Guide

COLOR NUMBER	COLOR
991	■ White

DMC Thread Guide

COLOR NUMBER	COLOR
Blanc	■ White
3045	▨ Yellow Beige, dark (or color to match felt)

Note: White thread is shown as black on the template.

Transfer the designs and embroider

Copy the template, enlarging it 127%. Transfer 2 of each of the heart designs to 6 of the pieces of felt using an iron-on transfer pencil or dressmaker's chalk carbon paper (see Transferring Designs, page 16). Stitch the project, following the colors and stitches indicated in the diagram. Refer to Finishing (page 154) to clean and press the hearts.

Finish the hearts

1. Trace the outline of the heart shape onto each cardboard piece and cut out all of the hearts, making sure the cut edges are fairly smooth.

2. Pin each embroidered felt piece to a plain felt piece and cut out both pieces at the same time around outside of the embroidered heart, leaving a ¼" (6mm) margin. Add a small dab of glue to 1 side of a cardboard heart and stick it to the plain felt heart, centering it evenly. Add a dab of glue to the center top edge of the cardboard heart and attach 1 short edge of a length of ribbon, letting the long end dangle out of the top of the heart. Add a small dab of glue to the center of the cardboard heart and press the embroidered felt heart, right side up, centering it evenly on the cardboard. Go easy with the glue here; you don't want it to soak through the felt, just hold things in place while you stitch the pieces.

3. Using 2 strands of color 3045 (Yellow Beige, dark) and small blanket stitches, stitch around the heart through both layers of felt, and the ribbon, enclosing cardboard inside. Repeat for all 6 hearts.

Make the mobile

1. Tie the remaining 6 lengths of ribbon to the edges of the grapevine wreath, spacing them evenly around the circumference. Gather up the ends of the ribbons to form the hanger; tie a small piece of floss tightly around all 6 of the ribbon ends, bunching them together about 2" (5cm) from the ends of the ribbons.

2. This next step is easier if you can hang your mobile from a hook, or have someone hold it for you: Tie each of the six hearts around the circumference of the wreath between the hanger ribbons, staggering the length of alternating hearts.

3. When everything is balanced, tighten the knots, and trim the ends of the ribbon. Use a scrap of ribbon to tie around the point where you used the floss to secure the hanger ribbons; it'll look prettier. Hang and enjoy!

Gingerbread Heart Mobile template
Use 1 strand of wool and 2 strands of floss throughout.
See page 14 for stitch abbreviations.
Enlarge template by 127%.

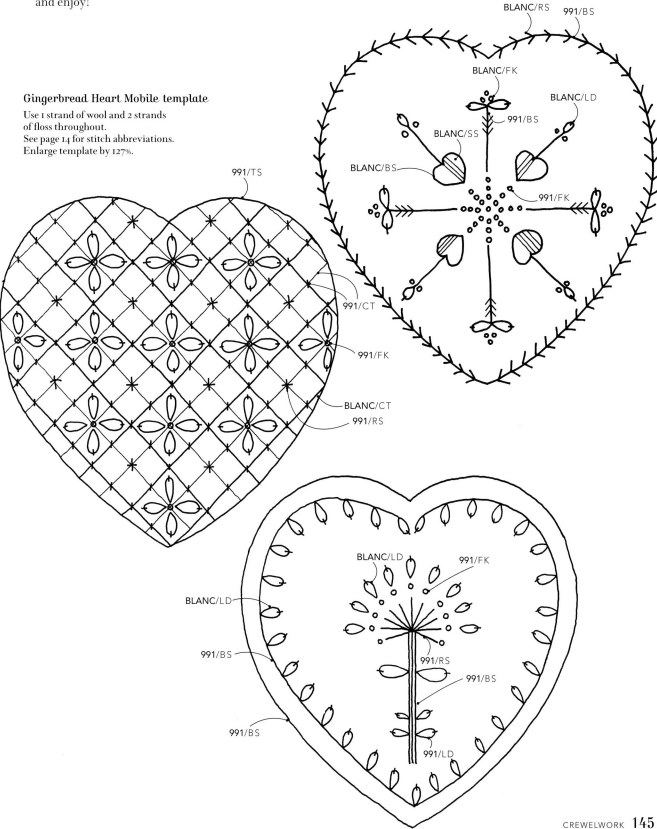

house

8582W
Terrazzo Gray

Retain this Portion
as a Reorder Reminder.

8582W
LRV 57

A

Appendices

Illustrated Stitch Guide

Running Stitch

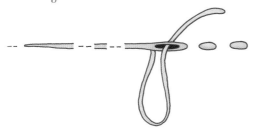

Running stitch is a simple outline stitch, and easy to master. Working from right to left, weave the point of the needle in and out of the fabric evenly, picking up several stitches, then pull the thread through.
To gather fabric, make running stitches along the seam to be gathered, then pull up the thread at each end, bunching up the fabric between the stitches.

Backstitch

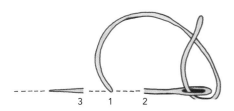

Backstitch is a commonly used outline stitch, making a straight, narrow line. Working from right to left, bring the needle up through fabric (1), insert it a short distance behind (2), and bring it up an equal distance in front of the point of entry (3). To make the next stitch, insert the needle back into 1, and bring it out an equal distance from the end of the new stitch.

Stem Stitch

Stem stitch makes a softer, more rounded outline than backstitch, and is frequently used on the stems of flowers and plants. Working from left to right, and keeping thread always on the same side of the needle (to the outside, if working around a curve), bring the needle out through fabric, insert at 1, and bring out a half-stitch behind the initial exit point, at 2.

Satin Stitch

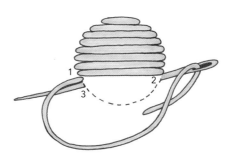

Satin stitch is an elegant, shimmery filling stitch that covers an area with smooth, closely placed straight stitches. It takes some practice to master. Working from left to right, bring needle up through fabric (1), down directly across from 1 (at 2), then up very close to but below initial exit point (3). For further control, do this stitch with a stabbing method, bringing the needle to the front and the back of the fabric in separate motions, rather than running the needle under the fabric and bringing the point out before pulling thread through.

Padded Satin Stitch

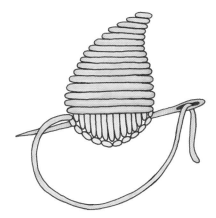

The padded satin stitch is a variation of the satin stitch that has a slightly raised quality, and reflects light more dramatically. To work it, first outline the shape you are filling with backstitches, then inside the backstitches, work a layer of satin stitch perpendicular to the direction you want the stitches of your final layer to lie. Then work a final layer of stitches over the sub-layer, being careful to completely cover all previous stitches.

Fly Stitch

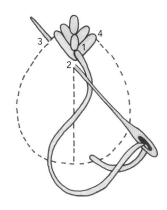

Fly stitch is my favorite leaf-filling stitch. To work, make a straight stitch to start at tip, then bring the needle up at point 1 and go down at 2. Bring needle up at 3, and insert at 4, directly across the leaf; bring up at hole made at 2. Carry the thread under the needle and pull through. To make the next stitch, insert needle directly below carried thread, placing stitches close together. Alternately, when making next stitch come up slightly beyond carried thread, creating a more open look.

Long and Short Stitch

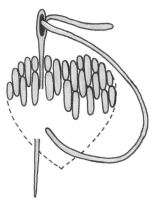

Long and short stitches are, as their name implies, satin stitches of different lengths used to fill an area. They are especially effective when used to move from one shade of a color to another, and help create a natural illusion of colors blending. To work, create a row of stitches alternating long and short. You can change color on the second row, and work long stitches into the ends of the first, staggering them alternately, ending with a row of short stitches as the shape is filled.

Chain Stitch

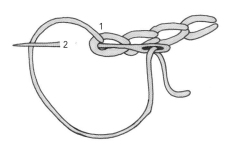

Chain stitch is so versatile—it can be used as an outline stitch, a filling stitch, or as an individual flower petal (see Lazy Daisy Stitch, page 150). A row is made by working a chain of loops in a line, with each link starting and ending in the previous link. To work, bring needle out at point 1, then, carrying thread under needle, insert needle back into or very close to point 1 and bring it out at 2. Pull thread through, keeping chain link flat. Repeat, always inserting needle into the hole made by the emerging thread of the same stitch. To end a row of stitches, take a small stitch over the last chain link to tack it down.

French Knot

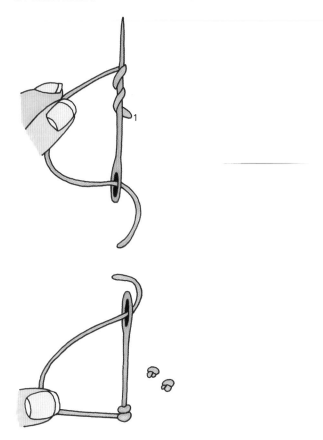

The French knot is a small, innocent-looking stitch, but it can take some practice to get it right. When my friend Lori finally "got" it, she said she wanted to tell me immediately (I'd shown her a week or so before, and she'd been practicing). Unfortunately, she was on a San Francisco city bus at the time, so only the other passengers were able to share in her jubilation (and I do believe she did attempt to elicit their enthusiasm). I was sorry to have missed it, because finally mastering the French knot is big news, and only those who've been successful can hoot and holler in the way such success deserves, and I would've whooped it up.

To work it, bring needle up at 1. Holding the thread taut with your left hand, wrap the thread around the needle clockwise twice. Insert the needle very close to point 1, and holding the thread tight against the needle with your left thumb and forefinger, pull the needle and thread through the knot gently.

Lazy Daisy Stitch

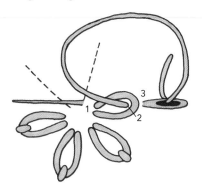

Also called the detached chain, this stitch is worked as the chain stitch but with each link tacked down, and the needle brought out at any place on the fabric. It is frequently used to make small flower petals. To work, bring needle out at point 1, then, carrying thread under needle, insert needle back into (or very close to) point 1 and bring it out at 2. Pull thread through, keeping chain link flat, and then take a small stitch over the chain link to tack it down (3). Bring the needle out wherever you desire to make the base of a new petal.

Blanket Stitch

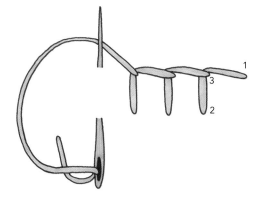

The blanket stitch can be both decorative and functional. It can be used to join pieces of fabric together or to finish a raw or folded edge. When it is worked close together, it creates a small ridge that can be used to outline a filled shape. To work, bring needle out at 1, insert at 2 (below and to the left), then come out at 3, directly above point 2. Pull thread through, carrying it under the needle. Work subsequent stitches the same way, keeping height of stitches even.

Couched Trellis

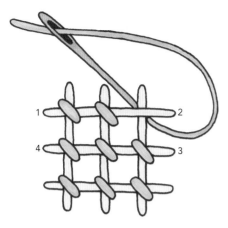

A couched trellis is made up of long stitches that cross each other to form a lattice, the intersections of which are held down by small slanting stitches. To form the lattice, start at the center of the shape: Bring the needle up at 1, go across the shape and down at 2. Bring the needle up at 3, down at 4, and continue spacing stitches evenly in this way (on either side of the first, centered stitch) until the shape is crossed in one direction. Then lay vertical stitches over the horizontal ones the same way. (The lattice does not have to be square; the foundation stitches can be at an angle to each other, as long as all stitches going in the same direction are parallel.) Then take small slanting stitches (or cross stitches) at each intersection.

Cross Stitch

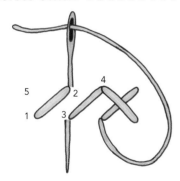

Cross stitches are made of two straight stitches of equal length, crossed perpendicularly. They can be worked in rows or individually, depending on the needs of the area to be filled—the important thing is that the stitches crossing on top all cross in the same direction. To work in a row, bring the needle up at 1, insert at 2, come up at 3, insert at 4, continuing in this way across row. At the end of the row, work back, crossing the stitches in the opposite direction.

To work individually, bring the needle up at 1, insert at 2, come up at 3, insert at 5 and pull the thread through.

Double Cross Stitch

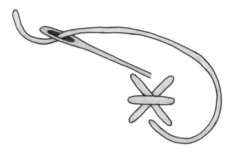

This stitch is just two cross-stitches that overlap. To work, complete a cross stitch, and then center another over it, rotating the top cross 45 degrees.

Woven Circle Stitch

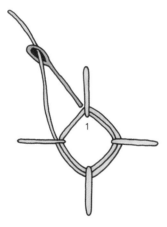

The woven circle stitch works best on gingham, where the woven circle encloses a white or colored square. To work, create four straight stitches around a single square of gingham. Bring the needle up at 1, then wrap the thread around the square going under all four legs of straight stitches; repeat. To finish, insert the needle under the first straight stitch, where thread originally exited.

General Sewing Techniques

Making a Square Bottom

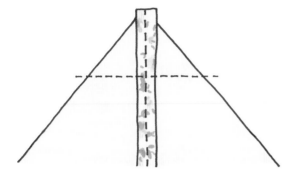

Making a square bottom on a bag is one of those things that's easier to do than to explain. Once you get the hang of it, though, you'll see there's nothing to it.

1. With the right sides of the bag pieces together, machine-sew the side and bottom seams of the bag (leaving an opening in the bottom seam to turn the bag, if necessary).

2. Keeping the wrong side out and the side seam facing you, stick your hand into the bag, toward one corner. With your other hand, push the side seam flat, pressing it against the bottom seam, creating a point with the corner of the bag as its apex. (Remove your hand from the bag.)

3. Keeping the side seam flat against the bottom seam, measure the required distance from the point and draw a line across the corner, perpendicular to the side seam (see illustration above).

4. Machine-sew across the corner on the line. Repeat all steps for the opposite corner of the bag. Turn the bag right side out and push the points toward the bottom center of the bag.

Whipstitch

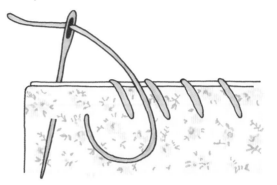

This is one of the simplest ways to attach two pieces to one another. Insert the needle from the back edge of the fabric to the front. Keep the needle at a diagonal to move from right to left along the seam.

Hemstitch

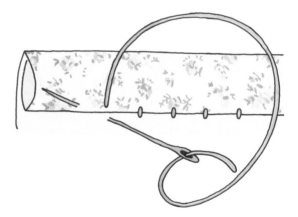

Knowing how to hem by hand is a great skill to have. After folding the hem up, secure it by working from right to left, bringing the needle and thread through the hem edge. Make a tiny stitch, catching only a couple of threads of the front of the piece. Then slide the needle under the hem about ¼" (6mm) to the left, just catching the hem above the fold.

When two hemmed edges meet at a right angle, the prettiest way to join the edges is to create a mitered corner. Trimming and folding a corner in this way reduces bulk and provides a tidy finish.

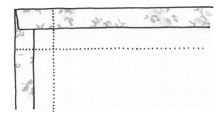

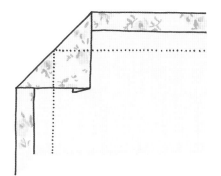

1. With the fabric wrong side up, turn in ¼" (6mm) of each edge and press. Then fold in each edge again along hemlines (the dotted lines in the drawing, above). Press, then unfold only the second set of folds.

2. Turn down the corner so the edges are parallel with the hemlines and the corner fold lies diagonally across the intersection of the hemlines.

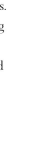

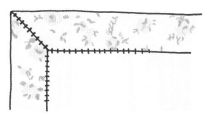

3. Trim off the corner, leaving a ¼" (6mm) allowance. Fold in the edges along the hemlines.

4. Sew the turned edges of the hems together either by hand, with hem-stitch (opposite) or by machine.

Finishing

In needlework lingo, "finishing" refers not just to the actual act of completing your project, but also to all the little tweaks and treatments you give it to make it look its best. It takes a little extra effort to finish a project properly, but trust me—it's time and energy well spent.

Cleaning

All the effort you put in to stitching a project shouldn't be diminished by grubby fingermarks or dirt smudges. It goes without saying that your hands should be as clean as possible when you're embroidering–wash them often, and try not to pet the dog too much between stitches (though that's hard, I know). The cleaner you can keep your work, the better.

If your finished piece looks a bit dingy by the time you've finished off that last thread, you may want to wash it gently before sewing it into its final form or framing it. Remember that you should only wash fabrics and threads that are washable to begin with–crewelwork is not a good candidate for soapy soakings, as the wool fibers can mat together, or "felt." If you're washing a piece embroidered with cotton floss on cotton fabric or linen, give it a swish in a clean basin filled with cool water and a bit of mild detergent. Never scrub, just swish, then rinse well. When rinsing, never wring. Roll the piece in a clean white towel to soak up excess water, and then lay flat to dry.

Pressing

If your piece needs pressing (and unless it was done on fairly heavy fabric it probably will), first lay a piece of white terry-cloth or a clean towel on your ironing board. The loops of this fluffy fabric will help keep your embroidered stitches from being crushed by the iron. Lay your embroidery face down, then use a clean white press cloth (a piece of flannel works well) and press with a warm iron. If necessary, you can dampen the press cloth a bit to help eliminate any wrinkles in your embroidered piece.

Framing

If you're going to frame your embroidery, roll your finished, pressed piece onto a cardboard tube (an old wrapping paper tube works great) and take it either to a professional frame shop or get brave and find a do-it-yourself shop in your neighborhood. I framed all of the pieces in this book myself and I have to say that, after putting all the work into designing and stitching each piece, it was very satisfying to do the final work of stretching and framing them on my own, as well.

A do-it-yourself frame shop will have lots of frames for you to select from–they'll help you measure your piece, determine how much of a border you need, weigh the pros and cons of using glass, and order or build your custom frame for you. They'll also cut a piece of foam core to the exact size needed to fit the frame, and show you how to stretch and pin the fabric evenly around it. Once the frame is ready, they'll also show you how to insert the embroidery, cover the back of the frame, and attach a hanging device. Easy, cheaper than professional framing, and a lot of fun, if you are a detail-oriented person who enjoys embroidering in the first place, I think you'll like doing this part yourself, as well. I did.

Resources

◇ ◇

Books

The history of embroidery is rich, varied, and fascinating. Much of the tradition exists only in very old illustrations and delicate, deteriorating finished pieces, stitched by humble domestic artists whose names we'll never know. Though contemporary designers are adding to the canon, some of my favorite inspirations come from hard-to-find, almost-forgotten sources. I hope these books provide you with a starting point from which to further explore both the history and the current trends in this beautiful craft.

Historical Designs and Alphabets

Bartholm, Lis. *Scandinavian Folk Designs.* Mineola, NY: Dover Publications, 1988.

Chapman, Suzanne E. *Early American Design Motifs.* Mineola, NY: Dover Publications, 1974.

Fisher, Eivor. *Swedish Embroidery: Anchor Embroidery Book #2.* London, United Kingdom: Clark and Co., 1953.

Geddes, Elisabeth, and Moyra McNeill. *Blackwork Embroidery.* Mineola, NY: Dover Publications, 1976.

Grafton, Carol Belanger, Ed. *79 Decorative Alphabets for Designers and Craftspeople.* Mineola, NY: Dover Publications, 1981.

—. *400 Floral Motifs for Designers, Needleworkers, and Craftspeople.* Mineola, NY: Dover Publications, 1986.

Luciow, Johanna. *Ukrainian Embroidery.* New York: Van Nostrand Reinhold, Co., 1979.

Nichols, Marion, Ed. *Designs and Patterns for Embroiderers and Craftspeople.* Mineola, NY: Dover Publications, 1974.

Nielsen, Edith. *Scandinavian Embroidery: Past and Present.* New York: Charles Scribner's Sons, 1978.

Orban-Szontagh, Madeleine. *Traditional Floral Designs and Motifs for Artists and Craftspeople.* Mineola, NY: Dover Publications, 1989.

Szalavary, Anne. *Hungarian Folk Designs.* Mineola, NY: Dover Publications, 1980.

Van Den Beukel, Dorine, Ed. *4000 Monograms.* Amsterdam, The Netherlands: The Pepin Press, 1998.

General Techniques

Bayard Marie-Noëlle. *Embroidery: Techniques and Patterns.* New York: Sterling Publishing, 2007.

Dardik, Helen. *Embroidery for Little Miss Crafty: Projects and Patterns to Create and Embellish.* Osceola, WI: Walter Foster, 2009.

Elder, Karen. *Embroidery: Techniques, Projects, Patterns, Motifs.* New York: Clarkson Potter, 1995.

Hart, Jenny. *Embroidered Effects: Projects and Patterns to Inspire Your Stitching.* San Francisco: Chronicle, 2009.

Nichols, Marion.
Encyclopedia of Embroidery Stitches, Including Crewel. Mineola, NY: Dover Publications, 1974.

Nicholas, Kristin.
Colorful Stitchery: 65 Hot Embroidery Projects to Personalize Your Home. North Adams, MA: Storey Publishing, 2005.

Norden, Mary.
Decorative Embroidery. Pleasantville, NY: Readers Digest, 1997.

Ray, Aimee.
Doodle Stitching: Fresh and Fun Embroidery for Beginners. Asheville, NC: Lark Books, 2007.

Cross Stitch

Foris, Andreas, Ed.
Charted Folk Designs for Cross-Stitch Embroidery: 278 Charts of Ancient Folk Embroideries from the Countries Along the Danube. Collected by Maria Foris. Mineola, NY: Dover Publications, 1975.

Kiewe, Heinz Edgar, Ed.
Charted Peasant Designs from Saxon Transylvania. Mineola, NY: Dover Publications, 1964.

Lindberg, Jana Hauschild.
Scandinavian Cross Stitch Designs: Over 50 Delightful Embroidery Designs from Norway, Sweden and Denmark. London, United Kingdom: Cassell, 1996.

Nichol, Gloria.
Cross-Stitch: Techniques, Projects, Patterns, Motifs. New York: Clarkson Potter, 1995.

Rankin, Chris.
Splendid Samplers to Cross-Stitch: 35 Original Projects. New York: Sterling/Lark, 1996.

Crewelwork

Burr, Trish.
Crewel and Surface Embroidery: Inspirational Floral Designs. Binda, New South Wales, Australia: Sally Milner Publishing, 2008.

Glenny, Mave.
An Introduction to Crewel Embroidery. London, United Kingdom: Guild of Master Craftsmen Publications, 1998.

Jeroy, Judy.
Creative Crewel Embroidery: Traditions and Innovations. Asheville, NC: Lark Books, 1998.

Shaughnessy, Katherine.
The New Crewel: Exquisite Designs in Contemporary Embroidery. Asheville, NC: Lark Books, 2005.

Embroidery Supplies and Fabric

I am lucky enough to live in a city that is blessed with a vibrant sewing community, and all of the supplies I used for the projects in this book came from local brick-and-mortar specialty and fabric stores I love and know well. When purchasing your threads, notions, and fabrics, I truly urge you to search out local retailers in your own neighborhood—not only are the proprietors of these shops almost always passionate sewers themselves (and hugely knowledgeable about their craft), they are also some of the friendliest and most helpful folks you'll ever know. That said, the internet has turned the craft world into its own (virtual) friendly neighborhood, and what you can't purchase locally, you can conveniently order from these sources.

Acorns and Threads
(cross-stitch supplies, evenweave fabrics, hand-overdyed embroidery floss)
4475 SW Scholls Ferry Road, Ste. 158
Portland, OR 97225
503-292-4457
www.acornsandthreads.com

DMC
(embroidery fabric and threads)
www.dmc-usa.com

Fabric Depot
700 SE 122nd Avenue
Portland, OR 97233
888-896-1478
www.fabricdepot.com

The Gentle Art
(hand-overdyed thread)
P.O. Box 670
New Albany, OH 43054
614-855-8346
www.thegentleart.com

JoAnn Fabric and Crafts
www.joann.com

Michaels Stores, Inc.
www.michaels.com

Needlework Corner
(embroidery supplies, fabric, crewel yarn, floss)
P.O. Box 473
Carbondale, IL 62903
618-529-5860
www.needleworkcorner.com

The Playful Needle
(crewel yarn and needlepoint supplies)
1103 SW Alder Street
Portland, OR 97205
888-825-4982
www.the-playful-needle.com

The Scarlet Letter
(historical sampler patterns and kits)
P.O. Box 397
Sullivan, WI 53178
262-593-8470
www.scarlet-letter.com

Framing

Dick Blick
www.dickblick.com

Frame Central
www.framecentral.com

The Great Frame-Up
www.thegreatframeup.com

Acknowledgments

Thank you, as always, to my remarkable families – the Ieronemos, the Smiths, and the Paulsons – and to my friends, who have always encouraged both my passions and my whims (and every single thing in between). Thank you especially for all the days you spent with me after my accident as I stitched my world back together, and got up on my feet again. I am here because you steadied my every step.

✦

Thank you to the sweetest, nicest, funniest, smartest, coolest, prettiest blog readers in the whole wide world. Posie Gets Cozy would not exist without you, and neither would my books. I love you guys.

✦

Thank you to Melissa Bonventre, Jennifer Graham, Betty Wong, Chi Ling Moy, Chalkley Calderwood, and everyone at Potter Craft, especially Erica Smith, who helps me put it all on the page. To my technical editor, Karyn Gerhard, who gets it all right. To my co-stylist, Andrea Corrona Jenkins, who helps me see. And especially to my agent, Colleen Mohyde, who is a dream come true. Thank you.

✦

My models are my friends: To Elizabeth Dye, Kristin Spurkland, Katie Harman Ebner, Tori Ebner, Arden Smith, and dearest Nicole Walker: Thank you for gracing these pages with your style, humor, patience, and honest beauty. Thank you sincerely to Darla Harman for so generously sharing her girls with me, and for helping to make our strawberry afternoon one I will never forget.

✦

To the generations of brilliant, unknown needleworkers who have inspired me, and to my Grandma Ieronemo: an angel, watching over me.

✦

Thank you from the bottom of my heart to Andy Paulson, who brightens every little corner until it shines: You light my world.

About the Author

Alicia Paulson learned to stitch as a child, but developed a passion for embroidery while recovering from a bad accident in 1998. She spends her days in her home studio sewing, crocheting, embroidering, and designing a small, ever-changing collection of original crafts and patterns called Posie: Rosy Little Things. She loves gingham, cuckoo clocks, rice pudding, Queen Anne's Lace, rosemaling, tiny calicos, vintage needlework books, taking photographs, taking walks in the woods, painting portraits, pioneer villages, smocked dresses, the Avett Brothers, Christmas movies, Indian food, peasant blouses, duffel coats, apple trees, and the little things in life, and she writes about all of them at her blog, Posie Gets Cozy. She is the author of *Stitched in Time: Memory-Keeping Projects to Sew and Share from the Creator of Posie Gets Cozy* (Potter Craft, 2008). Born and raised outside Chicago, she now lives in Portland, Oregon, with her husband, two-time Nurse of the Year Andy Paulson, R.N.; two comfort-obsessed cats; and the lovely, long-suffering Cardigan Welsh corgi, Clover Meadow Paulson. Find them all at www.AliciaPaulson.com.

Index